An Introduction to
Consulting Psychology

Fundamentals of Consulting Psychology Book Series

An Introduction to Consulting Psychology: Working With Individuals, Groups, and Organizations
Rodney L. Lowman

Transcultural Competence: Navigating Cultural Differences in the Global Community
Jerry Glover and Harris L. Friedman

Using Feedback in Organizational Consulting
Jane Brodie Gregory and Paul E. Levy

APA FUNDAMENTALS OF CONSULTING PSYCHOLOGY

An Introduction to
Consulting Psychology

WORKING WITH INDIVIDUALS, GROUPS, AND ORGANIZATIONS

RODNEY L. LOWMAN

AMERICAN PSYCHOLOGICAL ASSOCIATION • *Washington, DC*

Published by
American Psychological Association
750 First Street, NE
Washington, DC 20002
www.apa.org

To order
APA Order Department
P.O. Box 92984
Washington, DC 20090-2984
Tel: (800) 374-2721; Direct: (202) 336-5510
Fax: (202) 336-5502; TDD/TTY: (202) 336-6123
Online: www.apa.org/pubs/books
E-mail: order@apa.org

In the U.K., Europe, Africa, and the Middle East, copies may be ordered from
American Psychological Association
3 Henrietta Street
Covent Garden, London
WC2E 8LU England

Typeset in Minion by Circle Graphics, Inc., Columbia, MD

Printer: Maple Press, York, PA
Cover Designer: Naylor Design, Washington, DC

The opinions and statements published are the responsibility of the authors, and such opinions and statements do not necessarily represent the policies of the American Psychological Association.

Library of Congress Cataloging-in-Publication Data

Names: Lowman, Rodney L.
Title: An introduction to consulting psychology : working with individuals, groups, and organizations / Rodney L. Lowman.
Description: Washington, DC : American Psychological Association, 2016. | Series: Fundamentals of consulting psychology book series | Includes bibliographical references and index.
Identifiers: LCCN 2015031588| ISBN 9781433821783 | ISBN 1433821788
Subjects: LCSH: Psychological consultation. | Psychology, Industrial. | Organizational change. | Multiculturalism. | MESH: Counseling.
Classification: LCC BF637.C56 L69 2016 | DDC 158.3—dc23 LC record available at http://lccn.loc.gov/2015031588

British Library Cataloguing-in-Publication Data
A CIP record is available from the British Library.

Printed in the United States of America
First Edition

http://dx.doi.org/10.1037/14853-000

To Linda and Marissa with thanks and appreciation.

Contents

Series Editor's Foreword

Rodney L. Lowman

The field of consulting psychology has blossomed in recent years. It covers the applications of psychology in consultation to organizations and systems as well as individuals and teams. However, very few graduate training programs focus on this field of specialization, so consulting psychology roles are mostly populated by those who came to the field after having trained in other areas of psychology—including industrial–organizational (I-O), clinical/counseling, and school psychology. Yet such training is rarely focused on consulting psychology and psychologists, and graduate students have to learn through on-the-job training and by reading books and articles, attending conferences and workshops, and being mentored in the foundational competencies of the field as they seek to transition into it.

After a number of years of editing *Consulting Psychology Journal: Practice and Research*, the field's flagship journal, I felt that an additional type of educational product was needed to help those transitioning into consulting psychology. I therefore instigated a partnership of the Society of Consulting Psychology with the American Psychological Association (APA) and worked with an advisory board (initially consisting of Drs. Judith Blanton, Dale Fuqua, Skipton Leonard, Edward Pavur, Jr., and myself) to create a new book series describing the specific, fundamental skill sets needed to practice in this area of specialization. Our goal in this book series is to identify the major competencies needed by consulting psychologists and then to work with qualified authors to create short, accessible but evidence-based texts that will be useful as both stand-alone volumes and in combination with one another. The book is aimed at graduate students in relevant training programs, psychologists planning a transition into consulting psychology, and practicing professionals who want to add to their areas of expertise.

What constitutes fundamental skills in consulting psychology? The educational guidelines created by the Society of Consulting Psychology and approved by APA (2007a) and the *Handbook of Organizational Consulting Psychology* (hereinafter, *Handbook*; Lowman, 2002) provide useful starting points. Both of these contributions were organized around the concept of levels (individual, group, and organizational) as a taxonomy for identifying fundamental skills. Within those categories, two broad skill sets are needed: assessment and intervention.

As with many areas of psychological practice, the foundational skills that apply in one area may overlap others in the taxonomy. Interventions with individuals, as in executive coaching, for instance, usually take place in the context of the focal client's work with a specific team and within a specific organization, which itself may also constitute a client. Understanding the systemwide issues and dynamics at the organizational level usually also involves work with specific executives and teams. And multicultural/international issues suffuse all of our roles as consulting psychologists. The APA (2007a) guidelines and the *Handbook* (Lowman, 2002) concluded, properly, that consulting psychologists need to be trained in and have at least foundational skills and experience at the individual, group, and organizational levels, even if they primarily specialize in one of these areas.

As you learn more about consulting psychology through this book series, I hope you will come to agree that there is no more exciting or inherently interesting area of study today than consulting psychology. The series aims not only to cover relevant literature on timeless topics in consulting psychology but also to capture the richness of this work by including case material that illustrates its applications. Readers will soon understand that consulting psychologists are real-world activists, unafraid to work in real-world environments.

Finally, as one who trained in both I-O and clinical psychology, I should note that consulting psychology has been the one area in which I felt that all of my training and skill sets were both welcome and needed. This book series aims to make a difference by helping more psychologists join the ranks of qualified consulting psychologists who can help organizations and the individuals and teams within them meet some of their greatest needs: functioning effectively; bridging the individual, group, and organizational levels; and coping with the rapid expansion of knowledge and escalating competition and internationalization. Collectively, we can influence not only an area of specialization in psychology but also the world.

ABOUT THIS BOOK

As both series editor and author of this contribution to the series, I can say that this book provides a broad overview of the topics covered in more detail in the individual volumes. The organizing perspective of individual, group, and organizational approaches provides the basic framework, with assessment and intervention being the two basic professional competencies that need to be learned.

As an overarching view of a large and growing field, this book cannot provide depth to any one topic—that's not its purpose. Rather, it aims to introduce readers to a field that is an exciting area of practice for psychologists and other professionals. Although this book is mainly aimed at psychologists, other professionals can also benefit from it. In some chapters (e.g., Chapter 7), the focus is on ethics and standards that govern the practice of psychology in general and consulting psychology in particular. Psychologists have an obligation to practice ethically; those in other professions may be governed by different ethical considerations, but the issues (e.g., confidentiality, informed consent, conflicts of interest) are probably covered in applicable codes that usually say something similar to the codes of psychologists. The particular ethics standards I use in this book are those applicable to U.S. psychologists; those residing in other countries can use these as examples of applicable rules and laws, but they will need to identify the ethical and legal standards that apply to them. The *Standards for Educational and Psychological Testing* (American Educational Research Association, American Psychological Association, & National Council on Measurement in Education, 2014), however, are used worldwide, as they are the gold standard for all aspects of testing standards.

Consulting psychology is a field that is underrecognized and, when it comes to formal graduate training programs, underresourced. Some of the many reasons for this include (a) the fact that it covers a wide range of specific applications; (b) psychologists may come to consulting psychology from other areas of professional practice (e.g., clinical/counseling, I-O psychology); and (c) its research is often conducted by persons in a variety of specializations and settings, not just academics. The result is a practice-oriented field that has worked backward from practice to its foundational elements. I hope that this book series in general—and this book in particular—will encourage those aspiring to practice consulting psychology to get excited about this field. Much work is needed to help make our organizations and the individuals and groups within them become more effective and value driven, and to create that sweet spot in which individual, group, and organizational needs coalesce to the mutual benefit of all. Consulting psychologists who are able to understand, assess, and intervene with individuals, groups, and organizations are especially well equipped to meet this need.

An Introduction to
Consulting
Psychology

1

The Work of Consulting Psychologists

The work of consulting psychologists includes a variety of activities and specialization. Some focus mainly on individual assessment and coaching, others on team consultation or systemwide changes. Many work across a number of different levels. What they share is that they apply psychological knowledge to issues about which they advise others—or the group or organization as a whole—to work more effectively, to create conditions of high satisfaction and motivation, and to help people get along better with one another. Although the focus of this book is on consulting psychology in the context of work and work organizations, most of the principles also apply to other types of psychological consulting. Note that the primary role of consulting psychologists to advise others on how to do their jobs—not to do their jobs for them. (This can be difficult for many psychologists to learn because their training largely focuses on developing competency at the individual level. Typically, they study in-depth a

http://dx.doi.org/10.1037/14853-001
An Introduction to Consulting Psychology: Working With Individuals, Groups, and Organizations, by R. L. Lowman

somewhat narrow domain of knowledge that they apply to a consensually agreed-upon standard, rather than studying an array of areas.)

Broadly speaking, there are two major domains of knowledge (assessment and intervention) and three distinctive but overlapping levels to which consulting services can be applied (individuals, groups, organizations). Through skilled psychological assessment, the consulting psychologist can help the client (whether individual, group, organizational or some combination) understand what needs to be addressed for more effective functioning. Building on a broad knowledge of theory and research relevant to the particular problems or needs at hand, the psychologist helps empower clients to become more effective and more resilient.

The apparent conceptual simplicity of the consultation process belies the many moving parts and the complexity of theory and knowledge behind effective assessment and intervention. To identify appropriate assessment methods for the issue for which consultation is sought, the psychologist must have a wide-ranging diagnostic repertoire that encompasses individuals, groups, and organizations. To intervene requires matching what is learned through assessment with theory- and research-based intervention approaches that have diagnostic relevance and have demonstrated some likelihood of resulting in system or subsystem improvement. The rest is mostly art: translating knowledge and research into language that both reflects the knowledge base relevant to the particular issues at hand in a way that is both understandable and potentially impactful to the client or the client's representatives. With beginners, the process often appears mechanical and somewhat disjointed, with fully trained and experienced consultants, smooth and synergistic, and with master consultants, awe inspiring and life changing.

WHAT DO CONSULTING PSYCHOLOGISTS DO?

Working With Individuals

Often, a large part of psychologists' consulting practices involves work with individuals. Psychological assessments can be powerful and efficient ways of understanding what ails individuals in the context of their work;

what they are best suited to do; and who, among a group of individual candidates, is most likely to succeed in a defined work context. They can identify strengths and weaknesses relevant to career choice and change, assess fitness for work of persons with physical or mental disabilities, and assess the likelihood of behaving badly on the job, such as by stealing or by not following prescribed policies.

Consulting psychologists assess individuals using psychological tests, interviews, collections of perceptions from others in their clients' workspace, and self-assessments. They feed back the data collected to their clients or assessees and make recommendations about hiring potential candidates, firing and laying off employees, and managing problematic behavior on the job. They consider the ways in which individual behavior may be influenced by the groups or organizations in which people work. They often consult in the context of organizations in which they help identify the best people to do the important jobs. But they also work with individuals who seek the services of consulting psychologists for issues of career choice and change, who wish to be coached to be more effective in their work, and even those contemplating end-of-work-life transitions.

Individual-level consultation is not just done with persons experiencing problems. Many high-level, very successful executives hire consulting psychologists to help them sustain their effectiveness and improve in particular areas as they take on new roles. For example, as managers become executives, they must focus more on strategy and less on the day-to-day management of the organization. Consulting psychologists who work with such individuals must be fully competent in their skills, be able to build relationships quickly, and be prepared to be challenged. The overall focus in such cases is on enhancing success, not fixing problems.

In this book, case examples are provided to illustrate theory and practice. All cases are composites; none reflect actual specific cases, and all names and company names are fictional. The case material, however, is illustrative of the type of work with which consulting psychologists get involved. The first case is presented next.

Case 1: Individual-Level Issues at Scientific Dezigns

Phoebe worked in the sales department at Scientific Dezigns. She was not happy with the meeting she had just had with her boss. She masked her reactions, however, by trying to understand the perspectives of her boss, Rollie Rodgers, about what he described as being another instance of her poor interpersonal relations.

"Complaints have been made," he stated. She resisted the urge to say, "By whom and about what?", knowing that he would protect the identity of her detractors—likely her underperforming subordinates—in a way that seemed to take their side. "Jolly Rollie" was her pet nickname for her boss—who avoided contact, never wanted to rock the boat, and tried to preserve the veneer of camaraderie while never getting to the heart of the issues at hand. For those who didn't reach monthly performance objectives, however, Rollie was not so jolly.

Phoebe had loved her last boss, who was, like her, a well-trained scientist who was rational, logical, supportive, and not very political. Of course, that boss had not lasted long in the sales department of Scientific Dezigns. Sales were acceptable, but with company transitions and a merger, the last boss went to another subsidiary, and there was no job there for her to follow. She was quietly looking and biding her time with a boss whom she did not respect and two new male coworkers, neither of whom she either wanted or respected, and who seemed to be out to do her in.

Perhaps most galling of all was that Rollie had stated that Phoebe needed to visit the company's consulting psychologist for some help with her "problems." "I've used him myself," he said in his good-old-boy drawl, but she later learned that what he had neglected to mention was that he had "used him" only to make the referral about a manager who "was sorely lacking in the people skills department." The discussion with Rollie about a referral had not gone well, and although she would have preferred to visit a recruiter rather than a shrink, Phoebe was place bound until her 16-year-old son completed high school. With the recession, higher level jobs were not that plentiful.

Crisp, courteous, and contained, Phoebe always tackled unpleasant things she did not want to do by jumping into them quickly, rarely letting ambivalence set in. Yet, she had little stomach for discussing directly the anonymous attributions made about her and little interest in confronting the subordinates who could not be bothered to come directly to her with their concerns. Although she had her suspicions about who was complaining—two supervisees to whom she had to give less than positive feedback about their performance the previous week—she felt it was useless to address these individuals directly when she had no direct evidence of their complaints.

Phoebe listened to the psychologist's overly soothing voice on his voicemail and hung up, deciding instead to send him an e-mail that said, "Mr. Rodgers has suggested I contact you to discuss his perception that my interpersonal skills needed work. I am agreeable to meeting with you. Phoebe Kurstan." To the point and clear—and only mildly suggestive of the hostility and anxiety of which not even she was aware. Many in the office, however, interpreted her ambience of neutrality as coldness and disinterest.

For the consulting psychologist, the goals of meeting with such an individual client are complex. Why, other than the "recommended" referral, is Phoebe seeking help at this time? Is she motivated to work on the issues that caused the referral or is she just "going through the motions"? What was the "real" purpose of the supervisor's referral? Would the client authorize the psychologist to talk with her supervisor? Is the prospective client in the right career? Is she in the appropriate job? How well could she engage in a coaching relationship?

Working With Groups

Consulting psychologists work not just with individuals but also with groups. Groups are simply collections of individuals who have interrelationships with one another and who have some common purposes that bind them together. In the case of work groups, members typically have relationships with people that exist over time. They work together in some defined way to perform a productive function or task. But they also consist of people who have personal feelings for, and relationships with, one another. They like some members of their groups more than others, their feelings may vary over time, and they cooperate more with some people than others.

Because the individuals in work groups are discrete people, they also bring with them identities that influence not just their personal lives but also their work lives and how they react to events in the workplace. For example, individuals are members of gender, racial/ethnic, age, sexual orientation, religious/non-religious, and immigration status groups. Persons of color, for example, may be sensitive to perceived criticism, those with strong religious identities who work in scientific companies may feel they have to hide their beliefs, and young people may feel that existing processes are hopelessly outdated. But these identities can also create internal conflicts in their intersection, for example, a gay, Black, older, religious, scientist may compartmentalize some of these identities in the workplace.

Groups can consist of people who work face-to-face, or they may be virtual groups composed of individuals who are not colocated (see Purvanova, 2014). Sometimes these virtual teams may consist of people who are located in different countries or, in a large company, they may be people in the same building or city who rarely see one another in person. Although the same issues of norms, getting along with one another, social loafing, and managing affect can occur in virtual as occur in contiguous teams, they may take different forms and may need to be addressed differently depending on the circumstances.

Usually, groups have leaders. The leader is responsible for the team's working together to achieve its mission. Leaders come in many different types, and they may be the source of group cohesion and effectiveness, or they may be divisive (Filho, Tenenbaum, & Yang, 2015). Unofficial leaders also emerge in the group, including leaders of the group's socioemotional functioning. Different group leaders may assume leadership roles at different times and for different purposes.

Work teams may also be embedded in a network of other teams (e.g., manufacturing, marketing, sales), and such teams may experience difficulties from within the team or between teams in getting along with one another. One group, say sales, may blame another group, say manufacturing, for not delivering the product on time, who then in turn may feel that the sales group made overly optimistic promises about delivery dates.

And members of a work group come and go while the team stays intact—that is, the social entity can exceed the life of its individual members. This also means that when members leave a group, their losses must be dealt with, and as new ones arrive, they must be assimilated. In some groups, those changes are facilitated by formally celebrating the contributions of the member to the group and sending them off with best wishes. Others do not formally recognize departures and leave to the gossip mill the processing of feelings—good and bad—associated with the loss. When group members leave after having been promoted to higher levels, some members may be proud that the person has risen to a more influential position, but others may be jealous and believe that the promotion was unjustified. When work team members' services are terminated, others in the group may think that the terminations were unjustified and they might fear for the security of their own position.

In short, the many moving parts of work groups and teams means many opportunities for consulting psychologists to help them run more efficiently. These kinds of phenomena also highlight the importance of consulting psychologists understanding both individual and group dynamics, regardless of their areas of specialization.

Case 2: Group-Level Issues at Scientific Dezigns

The senior executive team on which Rollie Rodgers served was not a place for camaraderie. Scientific Dezign's CEO, Bruce Waltham, and his six direct reports (including Rodgers) met weekly for an hour and a half, but this was not the venue in which many real decisions got made. Rather, the meetings were for the sharing of information and blame, and Waltham imparted both in equal measure, edging slightly to the latter.

Rodgers was always frustrated in these meetings, but he rarely let it show. He could be counted on to add small, judiciously chosen, bits of humor to the conversation at hand, particularly when tensions threatened to surface, but otherwise he stared politely at the committee's chair and nodded slightly, suggesting affirmation but possibly masking his real reactions.

Relationships among members of this group were competitive, and a "CYA" norm had emerged over time. The concern with attributing blame had created a culture for the group in which few felt safe but subtle jibes and macho-like comments prevailed on those occasions when the silence was broken by someone other than the CEO. Truth be told, no one liked those meetings, but no one had the courage to confront the CEO or the group itself.

A consulting psychologist contemplating work with a group such as this would need both a reason and an invitation to intercede. Interventions with a group whose members and leaders are unhappy with their way of relating to each other or whose results are not up to expectations are difficult, but at least there is some leverage with which to work since there are strong pressures to change. Assuming group members had some motivation to identify and name the issues and to work toward change, the intervention might use a process approach (e.g., Schein, 1998) in which members of the group identify their preferred ways of relating versus what they currently were experiencing. Alternatively, a goal-focused approach might place more emphasis on the problematic outcomes. Individual interviews with members of the group might precede efforts at the group level.

Working With Organizations

When they run smoothly, organizations may seem to the outsider—or even to some of those inside the system—as if they are almost automated entities. For example, a machinery-intensive company such as a paper mill takes trees; converts them to pulp; and removes the water from the pulp using chemical processes and heavy equipment, which ultimately converts the pulp mass to paper used in newsprint, for stationery, greeting cards, toilet paper, and so on. When the machines are running well, they do so with great precision and the employees and supervisors seem at the time not to be very busy. But when the machines shut down for mechanical or other reasons, as they often do, the employees immediately jump into action and the climate becomes more frenetic than laid back. The costs of idle time on very expensive machines are considerable. Similarly, work organizations from the outside often look more stable than they really are. Few companies, for instance, in the private sector survive 75 years (De Geus, 2002a; see also Levinson, 2009). As De Geus (2002b) noted,

> The average life expectancy of a multinational corporation—Fortune 500 or its equivalent—is between 40 and 50 years. This figure is based on most surveys of corporate births and deaths. A full one-third of the companies listed in the 1970 Fortune 500, for instance, had vanished by 1983—acquired, merged, or broken to pieces. Human beings have learned to survive, on average, for 75 years or more, but there are very few companies that are that old and flourishing. (para. 2)

And those of us who lived through the financial meltdown of the past decade may remember the once-powerful corporations Goldman Sachs, Enron, Bear Stearns, Montgomery Ward, MCI, Washington Mutual, Countrywide, and Tyco. All of these were once-powerful, apparently sound, companies that were found to be malfunctioning and ethically challenged and in short order ceased to exist or were absorbed by other companies.

In large and specialized organizations, people's work may be relatively isolated from that of others in the organization. Yet, their collective fates are tied to the effectiveness with which they can get their work done and the success of the organization in fulfilling its mission. They also depend on the appropriateness of that mission in a constantly changing environment. Thus, the organization consists of a complicated system with many different parts that must interact successfully with its environment to successfully fulfill a purpose. And of course the greater the need and the more positive the outcomes associated with fulfilling that mission (profits, etc.), the more competition there is likely to be found in the environment and, hence, the more need to compete effectively with other organizations.

Let's consider a specific industry: commercial aviation. Each airline has huge investments in equipment and makes its money only when planes fly. But the planes must first and foremost operate safely, so airlines must manage the need for profits from planes being in the air with the need to follow a whole host of safety regulations in a highly regulated industry. When flights are delayed or cancelled, the airline must immediately manage a bevy of unhappy customers and get them on their way as quickly as possible. The capital that it takes to manage an airline is immense, the problems associated with managing a workforce constantly in motion complex and persistent, and the competition is keen (if shrinking through mergers and acquisitions). Such factors set the context within which consultation to that type of industry may occur.

People work from the context of their particular perch in the organization, especially in large organizations, and are rarely in a position to see the bigger picture or to understand the full complexity of the organization. In contrast, consulting psychologists are trained to understand the organization as a whole and are well situated to consider the bigger picture. As outsiders, they are often better equipped to see the organization in its complexity, to understand what may be driving the experienced problems, and to know how to address them.

Case 3: Organization-Level Issues at Scientific Dezigns

The board of directors of Scientific Dezigns was chaired by Peter "Pal" Johnston, head of a local small manufacturing company and a major stock holder. A man with less education than those who surrounded him, he had a reputation for micromanaging, tolerating no dissent, and having a quick temper. He was feared by those who knew his history of acting in anger and turning on a dime against anyone whom he perceived as having challenged his authority. As a result, the board meetings were highly structured, with more focus on decision making than on discussing the nuances of disagreement.

Several of the people he had fired had opened competing businesses in the same area; others, however, experienced traumatic personal reactions and never recovered fully. At the same time, some knew how to play Johnston, meeting with him privately at any opportunity to gossip and solicit his good will. He took their efforts to charm him to be genuine and thereafter took their sides on issues that arose. Were it not for his stock ownership, he would not have had anything to do with Scientific Dezigns and was quietly ridiculed among the scientists when they were among themselves. Those closer to him knew enough to fear him for his reputed bare-knuckled exercise of control; lack of cognitive complexity; and tendency to act immediately and think, if at all, later. His work sphere was small and controllable. His generous self-view was of being a man of action, oriented to customers, doing good in the world. But he had little understanding—and less interest—in knowing that others viewed him as being a bully and either avoided him or had learned how to use him to their advantage. Those who protested his behavior or tried even gently to confront it lived to regret it usually sooner rather than later. But as a major stockholder in the company with access to money, his abusive behavior was more or less tolerated by Waltham and his direct reports. The company needed his money and therefore tolerated his abuse.

Intervening at the organizational level is complicated by the interrelatedness of the parts—and the number of them. For-profit, but also many not-for-profit organizations, have multiple systems needed to get the work done—production, marketing, research, finance, human resources—and these can have a differential impact on operations. The board of directors is usually the policy-setting body of a corporation, and it directly controls the hiring and firing of the president or CEO of the organization, who in turn controls many aspects of the company. As with the group level, although plenty may be wrong with an organization, those who have the authority and power to bring in consultants to take action must be the ones to feel an organization's pain, or at least be aware of it.

Although a psychologist might conceptualize the problem in this case to be with the individual board chair and stock holder, from an organizational standpoint, that would lead to a very limited understanding of both the problem and how to intervene. Power-seeking and controlling individuals are common in high-level positions in organizations. The question is, "Is the organization adversely affected by how power conflicts are resolved?" Yet, over time, an organization is unlikely to succeed if dissent is not possible and if people are working and living in a climate or culture of fear. There is much material to work with at the individual and group levels, but if the problems experienced at the lower organizational levels stem from the power dynamics at the top, at some point that level too must be addressed.

Organizational-level intervention must work within the complexities of needing to assess across a range of issues and a large number of employees. Yet well-developed, scientifically anchored tools, such as well-designed and well-validated surveys (e.g., Church & Waclawski, 1998), enable the sources of organizational problems to be pinpointed and interventions planned. In this case, a survey of employee attitudes, including those of board members, might help to open up a conversation on corporate values and the organization's climate and, in turn, result in opportunities to identify a potential connection between a dysfunctional board and the climate in the rest of the organization. Such approaches should not be undertaken, however, without sufficient energy and engagement from key stakeholders at the various levels of the organization, which will be affected by the intervention. Organizational change is complicated, anxiety provoking, and sometimes painful and should not be undertaken without a solid commitment.

Consulting Across All Three Levels

Taken together, Cases 1 through 3 illustrate the interrelatedness of the three levels—individual, group, and organizational/systemic—in attempting to understand consulting dynamics. Because much of consulting psychologists' research is done at one level, they do not always see that behavior is not only a function of the psychological dynamics that the individual brings to the table but also a function of the environment with which they interact and their efforts to cope with that. Things are not always as they seem, or rather, they are often more complex than they seem. Constructions and conceptualizations appropriate to a single level (e.g., assumptions about the influence of personality variables on the behavior of managers) do not always help the psychologist know the full dynamics of what may be driving behavior—and of how to intervene to remediate it.

Where Consulting Psychologists Work

Because consulting psychologists may work primarily at the individual, group, or organizational level, or some combination thereof, they may be found in many different settings. Consulting psychologists are employed by work organizations (for-profits, hospitals, government organizations, nongovernmental organizations, schools, and consulting firms), or they manage their own private consulting firms of either a boutique or large scale. Development Dimensions International (DDI), for example, was started by one psychologist, Bill Byham, as a small consulting firm, but it grew into a large, internationally recognized, and highly successful firm working with top-level organizations. RHR International is another large-scale firm that was founded by a clinical psychologist, has multiple locations and affiliates in the United States and internationally, and has employed a number of psychologists who have either made careers there or gone on to other roles. Or, consulting firms can be smaller and more localized. TalentSmart, for example, based in San Diego, California, specializes in applications of emotional intelligence. The consulting firm Leadership Worth Following is based in Dallas, Texas, and specializes in executive assessment and coaching. Consulting psychologists may also be educators, teaching in colleges, universities, or private training programs. The Center for Creative Leadership, for example, has major offices in Greensboro, North Carolina; Colorado Springs, Colorado; and San Diego and employs psychologists as both trainers in their leadership training programs and coaching. Other consulting psychologists have part-time practices in consulting psychology while pursuing careers in other areas of psychology such as clinical and counseling, industrial–organizational, social, or school psychology.

Whatever their location, type of organization, or type of consultation provided, consulting psychologists must generally be prepared to work under time pressure. They must learn to rapidly understand the general characteristics of the situation in which they find themselves, ask the appropriate questions, and establish early on their credibility for the job at hand. The pace is fast, and executives, the usual decision makers, are demanding. If managers and executives do not make a connection with the consultant quickly or experience the consultant as competent, they will usually find someone else with whom to work.

If consulting psychologists simply try to respond to each situation in the same way using an approach with which they are familiar, they are likely to be incorrect a number of times. Psychologists are not trying to sell an unneeded product or approach, but they must nonetheless "sell" themselves and their general approach if they wish to have (and to retain) clients. If they arrive too quickly at a solution that does not fit the situation or shows no understanding of the situation at hand, they will experience difficulties. Thus the consulting psychologist must straddle the line between what it means to be a psychologist and the realities of surviving in the rough-and-tumble world of corporations and other types of work organizations. But if they do not retain their identity and ethical expectations of being psychologists, they will not be functioning as consulting psychologists, just as consultants of any stripe, plying their respective trades.

THE VALUES OF ORGANIZATIONS AND THE VALUES OF PSYCHOLOGISTS

Psychologists are trained in the science and practice of psychology and in the ethics of a profession committed to serving the greater good. As the "Ethical Principles of Psychologists and Code of Conduct" (hereinafter, "Ethics Code"; American Psychological Association [APA], 2010) describes,

> Psychologists are committed to increasing scientific and professional knowledge of behavior and people's understanding of themselves and others and to the use of such knowledge to improve the condition of individuals, organizations, and society. (Preamble)

They are expected to practice a science-based discipline and to put their clients' interests ahead of their own. They have restrictions on how they can market and advertise their services. And they must be skilled at managing complex client situations with multiple clients and those whose interests must be taken into account.

Organizations exist also to serve a productive purpose that has value in some marketplace (including the marketplace of ideas), but such purposes are unlikely to be the same, or to represent the same values, as those of many psychologists. Rather, organizations exist to serve a particular purpose, such as manufacturing, knowledge creation, or service delivery, through which they earn money and other rewards for their stakeholders. They are, of course, not obligated to behave in a manner consistent with the Ethics Code, although they have a number of laws and regulations that govern their behavior. To the extent that their leaders view their goals as being to promote the narrowly defined success of the organization (e.g., shareholders' dividends, quarterly profits) even when that pursuit comes at the expense of other goals or values (e.g., employee satisfaction and well-being), conflicts in role and values may arise with which the consulting psychologist will have to deal (see Lefkowitz, 2003; Lefkowitz & Lowman, 2010).

WHY CONSULTING PSYCHOLOGY IS EXCITING WORK

If the above examples of consulting psychology work appeal to you, it is likely that you will find a happy and professionally satisfying occupational home doing this type of work. Indeed, there is more money to be made here than in most areas of psychology (see, e.g., Blanton, 2007; O*NET, n.d.-c), but I argue that the reason to do it is to help to make a difference in organizations and in the lives of the individuals and groups within them.

For those excited by complexity, who thrive on addressing real-life problems in real time, and who care as much about strengths and optimization as dysfunction, consulting psychology is a remarkable area in which to practice. It also offers the opportunity to influence more people than applications of psychology that focus solely on addressing the needs of individuals. Whether in successfully addressing issues experienced by leaders (who in turn influence a number of employees, such as the CEO of a large company employing thousands or more) or helping to solve work group issues, psychologists who consult can make a significant difference.

FOR WHOM THE BELL DOES NOT TOLL

Consulting psychology is probably not the venue of choice for many mental health clinicians. What attracted them to psychopathology and individual-level functioning they may not find in assisting with the problems and issues of people who, for the most part, are typically concerned with work issues. Few clinical or counseling psychology programs have much to say about work and organizations and consulting. If taught at all, it usually occurs in the context of consulting to other mental health professionals on mental health issues. Passion for the subject matter is important in deciding whether consulting psychology is a good fit.

PLAN OF THIS BOOK

This book was written as an overview of the field of consulting psychology in the Fundamentals of Consulting Psychology book series. As such, it provides a broad overview of the field intended to help those just beginning their study of psychology, as well as those already practicing in other areas, to become excited about working in this area. Further training will be needed in the areas of specialization.

The "Guidelines for Education and Training at the Doctoral and Postdoctoral Levels in Consulting Psychology/Organizational Consulting Psychology" (APA, 2007a) provide a structure that is helpful as an organizing device, dividing the practice of consulting psychology into three levels (individual, group, and organizational) and two major activities (assessment and intervention; see Table 1.1 with some sample areas). This book makes use of that structure as its primary organizing device.

The remaining chapters of this book introduce major work activities at the various levels (individual, group, organizational) and then pro-

Table 1.1

Levels and Types of Activities in Consulting Psychology

	Levels		
	Individual	Group	Organizational
Type of Activity		Sample Activities	
Assessment	Career Assessment	Role Analysis	Culture Assessment
Intervention	Coaching	Tavistock Groups	Scanlon Plan

ceed to professional practice issues. Chapter 2 focuses primarily on the work of consulting psychologists at the individual level, examining how to help individuals build upon their strengths and abilities to improve performance and manage major career transitions. This chapter also covers other areas of assessment, such as screening potential job or promotion candidates and measuring employee psychopathology. Coaching, the most popular form of individual-level intervention, and various other intervention approaches are discussed. Chapter 3 looks at group-level assessments and interventions, such as evaluating work group dynamics (e.g., members' roles and communication patterns) and working with individual members and the team as a whole to improve group-wide performance and procedures. Chapter 4 reviews consulting psychology at the organizational systemic level, examining key theoretical models for assessing organizations as a whole, including its culture, and targeted interventions for improving various systems and subsystems. Chapter 5 covers leadership and demonstrates that the levels are often artificial boundaries, so it is important to know how they intersect and overlap. Chapter 6 introduces multicultural/international issues relevant to consulting psychology, such as addressing workplace discrimination, using diversity to improve organization-wide outcomes, and working with international companies. Chapter 7 reviews the Ethics Code (APA, 2010) and other professional guidelines that consulting psychologists should be familiar with. The final chapter, Chapter 8, looks ahead to provide suggestions for future work.

2

Consulting at the Individual Level

Consulting psychologists working at the individual-level fulfill two primary roles: (a) career and work-related assessments and (b) interventions with individuals to assist them with work-related issues. I use the term *issues*, depending on context, to mean a particular consulting objective, problems, or opportunities to help improve performance. Well-trained and experienced consulting psychologists perform all of these roles.

In the case of assessments, consulting psychologists evaluate individuals using psychological tests, observations, and other assessment devices, but their clients may also be the individuals themselves or others who contract for the consulting psychologist's services, such as employers who want individuals assessed for purposes that can include selection, career management, or determining fitness for duty. Interventions at the individual level can address a number of types of activities, including coaching, counseling

http://dx.doi.org/10.1037/14853-002
An Introduction to Consulting Psychology: Working With Individuals, Groups, and Organizations,
by R. L. Lowman

for work-related issues (e.g., procrastination, underachievement), providing feedback on coworkers' perceptions of the client, and helping managers and executives to improve their relationships with their subordinates.

To some extent, of course, the separation of interventions into the individual–group–organizational categories can be somewhat arbitrary, as helping to examine assessments and interventions in which an individual is the primary focus of the consultation. Clearly, in working with individuals in organizational contexts, the focal problems may necessitate also working at the group and organizational levels. Still, the client in the cases at issue in this chapter is more likely to be an individual. This chapter presents a few illustrative case examples.

ASSESSMENT AT THE INDIVIDUAL LEVEL

One of the things that psychologists, compared to other types of consultants, bring to their work is understanding the role and importance of assessment, often using psychological instrumentation. Yet, the question must still be raised: What is it that needs to be assessed by consulting psychologists and using which assessment instruments? Can the consulting psychologist learn a standard set of measures and apply them to a variety of situations?

Over the years, I have noticed that many psychologists trained in mental health issues often persist in using psychological assessment measures in which they were trained in graduate school without thinking much about what they are assessing, whether better instruments would suit the issue at hand, or even whether the particular instrument chosen has sufficient evidence of validity for the inferences for which the scores will be used (see American Educational Research Association [AERA], American Psychological Association [APA], & National Council on Measurement in Education [NCME], 2014; Putka & Sackett, 2010; Schmitt, Arnold, & Nieminen, 2010). It is important to use psychological assessments in appropriate ways and when it comes to consulting psychology applications this is particularly true. (See chapter 7 for further discussion.)

The results of relevant psychological assessments can be very powerful in quickly obtaining information about candidates for selection or promotion (see, e.g., Jeanneret & Silzer, 1998; Prien, Schippmann, & Prien, 2003), but it requires both time and discipline to be able to create an appropriate assessment ("diagnosis") program for a particular situation or individual. Some assessments are often driven more by what is popular and what de facto becomes a norm to use, without an understanding of limitations of method or the risks entailed.

The use of 360° feedback (360s) provides a good example. This type of assessment involves first having both self-ratings of various work-related performance issues along with those done by employees who are peers, subordinates, and bosses rate the individual, and then giving this feedback to the focal employee. On the one hand, this type of assessment is the norm in assessing executives to employ 360s (see, e.g., Gregory & Levy, 2015; Lepsinger & Lucia, 2009; Levy & Williams, 2004). On the other hand, 360s are fraught with problems and can be greatly misused, and poorly handled feedback can cause psychological problems and actually worsen rather than improve performance (Nowack & Mashihi, 2012; Vukotich, 2014). Consulting psychologists need to know how to administer and interpret the results of such assessments.

Because the purpose of the assessment must drive instrument selection, I begin there. In the next section, I discuss some of the common uses for assessments.

Career Assessments

Career assessments may be conducted for a specified and delimited purpose (e.g., "Should I attend law school or get an MBA?") or for broad questions (e.g., "What careers am I best suited for?"). Testing may or may not be needed with either example, but chances are it will be worth the time, effort, and money to do so, at least if the client is ready for that type of assessment. For instance, if parents think their teenage child should be assessed to become more "goal directed," less time and frustrating effort will be expended when the teen also thinks that assessment is a good idea.

In career assessment, the conceptual issue is to identify from thousands of potential occupations those for which the client is best suited. Career assessment that could cut through all the myriad of possible career paths and find the single one for which the client is best suited and that will enable her or him to live happily ever after in that career would be nice, but realistically such assessments do not exist—the choices are too many and the research relevant to combining across variables too limited. Rather, career assessment is best at helping the client narrow down a list of possible career paths—directions the client has thought about or is contemplating among realistic opportunities—and providing guidance about where the best fit might be within a particular career. For example, law, psychology, and medicine, among many other professions, are large and diverse with a number of specific career paths possible (see, e.g., O*NET, n.d.-b), some of which will be better fitting for some than for others. The typical variables on which clients will be assessed are occupational interests (Holland, 1997; Lowman, 1993b; Lowman & Carson, 2012), abilities (Lowman, 1991; Schmidt, 2014), and personality (Hogan, 2006; Hough & Dilchert, 2010).

In the ideal state, alignment of career with personal characteristics can result in a strong fit and sense of purpose. Wayne Dyer (2014), a popular author and self-help guru, put a religious spin on this and argues that people aligned with their purpose will be highly motivated and inspired, effortlessly pursuing their life's purpose and calling. He also noted that, too often, people are not able to identify for themselves what they are motivated by and passionate about, being too influenced by others' views of what they should or should not do with their lives and too easily derailed from their own purposes (Dyer, 2014).

Interest variables particularly speak to the emotional investment in which people will find work or avocational activities enjoyable and more (or less) effortless. Occupations attract people with common interest patterns (Holland, 1997). For example, people in medicine (see O*NET OnLine; http://www.onetonline.org/find/quick?s=physicians), accounting (http://www.onetonline.org/find/quick?s=accountants), managership (http://www.onetonline.org/find/quick?s=executives), and entrepreneurs (Almeida, Ahmetoglu, & Chamorro-Premuzic, 2014) often share common and differentiating interest types or subtypes (see also Chapter 6). Of course, the remarkable directions in which people's basic intelligence and other abilities can be applied (Schmidt, 2002) enable people to perform work about which they may not be passionate or inspired. The purpose of career assessment is to use the skills, knowledge, and wisdom of the psychologist to help the client find possible careers and work in which passion can match abilities and personality. Part of that task is to help the individual understand both the paths taken and not taken and to identify how course corrections may be needed. And the tools of the psychologist can be powerful in aiding the client to be more effective and purposeful in career choices and to realize that career change and development requires action on the part of the client and that inaction is itself a choice. As da Vinci (as cited in Edberg, 2010) famously put it "It had long since come to my attention that people of accomplishment rarely sat back and let things happen to them. They went out and happened to [do] things" (section 1, para. 2).

But whereas consulting psychologists often assess candidates for managerial roles, in conducting career assessments a broader array of abilities must be considered. For example, general intelligence (see Hunt, 2011) is important in many types of work, but imagine the not atypical situation in which the career assessee has aspirations in an artistic area, such as music, visual arts, and dance. Knowledge of a much broader spectrum of abilities is needed to be able to competently assess in such cases.

Use of tests is only one part of career assessment. The job is to help clients come to their own conclusions. The consulting psychologist uses the results of testing not to definitively declare outcomes as if a diagnosis of career misfit alone were enough to spur action but rather to help the client expand his or her repertoire of factual information that needs to be considered in making sense of the present unhappiness and inertia in not making changes. The tenor of the discussion is one of shared discovery and understanding (see, e.g., Savickas, 2011), helping to provide information that may help explain both barriers and opportunities. The goal also is to help the client have more options and more confidence and self-efficacy in moving forward with a better-fitting career path. When the client's current or desired directions are not well matched with his or her interests, abilities, or personality characteristics, the psychologist helps the individual understand the nature of the misfit and what might be needed (e.g., greater effort than others who pursue such careers, choice of a specialized area within a larger career path that is better fitting) to move in the espoused direction, or coaching and support in changing career directions to a better fitting course. It is, after all, not the psychologist's job to make career decisions for the individual but rather to coach the client using the powerful ally of assessment data to help the client.

Preemployment or Prepromotion Screening for "Best Fit" Candidates

Individual-level assessments for work-related issues assess clients for either specific positions (e.g., finalists for a city manager's position) or a generic job class (e.g., entry level manager). The consultant's role is to assess a group of individuals to identify the candidates who are best qualified and also to provide for the client and/or the individuals being assessed the pattern of strengths and weaknesses and possibly development plans.

Assessment at the managerial level may be generic, directed to a broad range of candidates, or may be specific, for a class of jobs, such as entry level managerial positions. Assessment centers (see Krause, Kersting, Heggestad, & Thornton, 2006; Thornton, Hollenbeck, & Johnson, 2010; Thornton, Rupp, & Hoffman, 2015) combine simulations (e.g., leaderless groups and in-basket tests that monitor the manager's day-to-day work) with traditional cognitive ability testing to identify best-performing candidates or simply the strengths and weaknesses of the evaluated candidates. In a multiple hurdles approach (e.g., Finch, Edwards, & Wallace, 2009), candidates must successfully complete various steps (e.g., resume review, cognitive ability tests, assessment centers) to continue on to the next ones and the finalists judged as to whether they are "best" or "fully qualified."

Case 4: Best and Brightest

A consulting psychologist was asked to evaluate three finalists for the position of chief financial officer of a medium-sized family-owned business. All three had been successful in their careers to date, and this position would offer the chance for a promotion. A job analysis was provided by the organizational client, which indicated they were particularly concerned about the goodness of fit with a family-owned business (none had worked at such a company before). Each candidate participated in an assessment process consisting of assessment of interests, abilities, and personality characteristics related to the position. Ability measures included a measure of cognitive ability appropriate for the college graduate level and above, a measure of financial knowledge, an in-basket geared to the assessment of prioritizing and managerial judgment related to financial management, and a leaderless group discussion. Personality measures encompassed job-related personality variables. Review of assessment results, combined with the results of the hiring official's input led to a prioritized list of recommendations of the order of the three candidates and a list of strengths and weaknesses for each of them in the context of the specific position. All three were judged to have had the minimal competencies needed for the position, but one was considered to be more likely to be successful in the specific family business context. The client combined the results of the assessments with the results of its own interviews including responses of those in the organization with whom the candidate would work. The consulting psychologist then worked with the company to help ensure a successful onboarding process for the selected candidate.

PREEMPLOYMENT OR ON-THE-JOB ASSESSMENT FOR PSYCHOPATHOLOGY

Psychologists' selection efforts must take account of applicable laws and regulations. Psychologists are sometimes called upon to screen job candidates for psychopathology. Such screening is either required or recommended for certain public safety jobs, such as pilots or police officers. Psychologists with backgrounds in clinical and counseling psychology but who have also trained in industrial–organizational (I-O) psychology may be particularly well qualified to consult on such projects. For example, few would want to fly in airplanes piloted by those who were not screened to weed out persons with acute, serious mental health problems that might affect their ability to safely fly the plane. (Highly publicized cases of pilots who have intentionally crashed planes, e.g., the 2015 crash of a German plane by a seriously psychologically disturbed but planful pilot, illustrate the importance of this work; see Kulish & Clark, 2015.)

As with most aspects of selection, however, the issues are more complicated than they first appear. Employers in the United States may screen for psychopathology or other conditions covered by the Americans With Disabilities Act (ADA) only when it is job relevant after postconditional offers of employment and only when administered to all employees in that class. The intent is to keep so-called disabilities from being bases for out-of-hand rejection before the abilities of the employee were considered. The ADA makes no requirement that persons with disability be made offers of employment—conditional or otherwise. Such individuals must demonstrate job proficiency. Because the review of job-related abilities and other characteristics, such as personality or interests, is made up front and without consideration of the disability, the argument is that persons with disabilities are given a better opportunity to be seriously considered for jobs. The ADA law also specifies that persons with disabilities must be given reasonable accommodations on the job if, with such adjustments, they are able to perform the job to an appropriate standard.

In the case of mental health disabilities, and depending on the job, certain conditions might be rule-out considerations (e.g., for security-related positions). Whether a person with a diagnosis of paranoid schizophrenia, controlled by medication, would be appropriate for a job as a commercial pilot might be differentially evaluated than for a technical position involving little work with others. These decisions are always made on an individual basis and care must be taken to balance the needs of the organization, the abilities of the individual, and the risks associated with the condition defined as a disability.

As an aside, I should also note that in the case of mental health conditions, decisions about employment are not once and forever. Some chronic mental health disorders do not manifest before a certain age, and some symptoms that have the potential to affect work performance may generally be controllable unless an employee ceases taking medication or his or her disorder changes over time. Employers need to be prepared to assess and address the needs of employees with mental disorders that arise over the course of employment. Pilots, for example, may be perfectly well adjusted at the time of their hire but later in their careers may, like anyone else, experience problems with depression or substance abuse that then may adversely affect their ability to fly.

As might be surmised, employment testing is a complicated undertaking, with many legal parameters and possibilities of lawsuits (see, e.g., Landy, Guttman, & Outtz, 2010). Consulting psychologists who work in this area need to be adequately trained in the laws and court cases associated with personnel selection or to work with psychologists and human resources professionals with the requisite knowledge and experience to set up, conduct, and if necessary, defend personnel selection decisions. Partnering with psychologists who specialize in aspects of I-O psychology related to selection may be appropriate when these competencies are not among the consulting psychologist's primary areas of expertise.

Still, properly trained consulting psychologists have many opportunities to be involved in assessments for selection. Feedback sessions with those selected to help them make appropriate use of the assessment results may be helpful. Providing onboarding and coaching services to assist with transitions into jobs, especially of those with special needs, can also be useful.

INDIVIDUAL-LEVEL INTERVENTIONS

Coaching

In general, coaching performed by consulting psychologists directly or indirectly centers on work-related concerns. These may focus on career choice or change; difficulties in performing the current work role; trouble getting along with others in the workplace including coworkers, superiors, or subordinates; and other challenges such as difficulty managing political issues. Other coaching issues relate to the intersection of personal and psychological concerns and work/career issues. Or, the person being coached may be at a point in the individual's career when more time is desired for home life or when family pressures are crowding out work-related ones.

Coaching today is in many ways similar to psychotherapy in its early decades. Psychotherapy also tapped into a nerve that led to widespread proliferation of many flavors and varieties, owned by no one profession, and its outcomes were scientifically evaluated by very few. Models and treatment were promoted by assertion, at least until researchers—especially psychology researchers—began to ask the outcome questions about what worked and what did not (see Smith & Glass, 1977). From that point forward, although "schools" of psychotherapy (e.g., psychodynamic, behavioral, cognitive) continued to exist, research focused more on the common factors in psychotherapy and which among those contributed to successful outcomes.

The nerve that coaching tapped was the socially approved opportunity for managers to seek and to receive help to perform their jobs better without having to define themselves as having "problems." Because coaching had already existed in athletics, it became a socially acceptable approach for managers (who, as a group, tend to be counterdependent; see Lowman, 1991, 1993a) to have a coach to make performance better. One did not have to have a problem to get better, just as few would begrudge or see as irrelevant an athlete working with a coach.

As psychologists came to the rapidly burgeoning territory of coaching, they did not cease to be psychologists. They remained concerned about whether coaching was sufficiently validated and were among the early contributors to the outcome literature (see, e.g., Grant, 2013; Kampa-Kokesch & Anderson, 2001; Kilburg, 2000, 2007a, 2007b). As of this writing, coaching is still in the early stages of attracting serious research. Grant (2013) recently attempted a comprehensive review of all studies up to that point that had a between-subjects design. He found only 26 studies, and they varied widely in quality and, arguably, relevance. Clearly, the field is ripe for further research, but as with most applied research, it is very difficult to conduct fully controlled studies in actual organizations.

Consulting psychologists bring to the field of coaching an understanding of people in their social context, the concept of levels (individual, group, organizational), and an understanding of the role and importance of integrating research and practice by using evidence-based approaches. As a group, however, they tend to be less knowledgeable about the workings of business, the norms and values of managers, and the expectations of employees in usual work settings. (After all, they chose to become psychologists, not managers.) And consulting psychologists who trained in I-O psychology are steeped in the importance of job relatedness (Pearlman & Sanchez, 2010), something that is absent from the training of most clinical and counseling psychologists. Once again, however, the vulnerability of those coming from backgrounds in clinical/counseling psychology relates to their lack of training in organizational issues; the vulnerability of I-O psychologists is their lack of training in individual-level work and in counseling techniques.

Classifying Coachable Concerns

Currently, there exists no theory driven or empirically derived comprehensive taxonomy of coaching-related issues or problems to which the coaching is directed. And often (too often) the approach to coaching follows the preference of the coach for a particular model (e.g., behavioral, psychodynamic, mindfulness, positive psychology) rather than a problem-by-intervention approach based on well-validated evidence. Partly, this reflects the absence of a consensually agreed-upon taxonomy of issues to be coached and partly it is influenced by the scarcity of empirical outcome research.

In an earlier book, *Counseling and Psychotherapy of Work Dysfunctions* (Lowman, 1993a), I developed a taxonomy of issues that can occur in the work role (see Exhibit 2.1; Lowman, 1993a). These included patterns of undercommitment; patterns of overcommitment, anxiety and depression in the workplace, and work issues of the creatively talented. Patterns of undercommitment, e.g., addressed issues of underachievement and the creatively talented often suffer from patterns of depression and mania, narcissism, and substance abuse. The taxonomy then identified particular syndromes or patterns within each of these areas (e.g., undercommitment problems included procrastination).

Peterson (2011) indirectly addressed problem type by suggesting a taxonomy of coaches. This approach to how coaches add value includes providing (a) feedback directed to increasing awareness, (b) insight and accountability, (c) specific skills development, and (d) personal development and process understanding. Although this taxonomy does not address problems for which help is sought, it does assist indirectly by considering what different types of coaches actually do to assist their clients.

An advantage of a taxonomy of concerns to which coaching can be applied is that it enables agreement on terms about the nature of the issues being addressed by various approaches to coaching. Without

Exhibit 2.1

Toward a Clinically Useful Taxonomy
of Psychological Work-Related Dysfunctions

I. Determining the relation between psychopathology and work dysfunctions
   A. Affecting work performance
   B. Not affecting work performance
   C. Affected by work performance
   D. Not affected by work performance
II. Disturbances in the capacity to work
   A. Patterns of undercommitment
      1. Underachievement
      2. Temporary production impediments
      3. Procrastination
      4. Occupational misfit
      5. Organizational misfit
      6. Fear of success
      7. Fear of failure
   B. Patterns of overcommitment
      1. Obsessive–compulsive addiction to the work role ("workaholism")
      2. Type-A behavioral pattern
      3. Job and occupational burnout
   C. Work-related anxiety and depression
      1. Anxiety
         a. Performance anxiety
         b. Generalized anxiety
      2. Work-related depression
   D. Personality dysfunctions and work
      1. Problems with authority
      2. Personality disorders and work
   E. Life role conflicts
      1. Work–family conflicts

Exhibit 2.1

**Toward a Clinically Useful Taxonomy
of Psychological Work-Related Dysfunctions (*Continued*)**

F. Transient, situational stress
  1. Reactions to changes in the work role (e.g., new job)
     whose impact on the work role is time limited
G. Other psychologically relevant work difficulties
  1. Perceptual inaccuracies
III. Dysfunctional working conditions
  A. Defective job design (role overload, ambiguity, etc.)
  B. Defective supervision
  C. Dysfunctional interpersonal relationships

Note. From *Counseling and Psychotherapy of Work Dysfunctions* (pp. 43–44), by R. L. Lowman, 1993, Washington, DC: American Psychological Association. Copyright 1993 by the American Psychological Association.

---

that, case study and empirically-based outcomes-research study would have to describe idiosyncratically the concerns being addressed (see, e.g., Lowman, 1993a, 2007), leaving uncertainty about whether the clients all in the experimental group(s) were working on comparable issues. As one example, Grant's (2013) summary of five coaching outcome studies included participants in a medical college admission course (Taylor, 1997), substance abuse professionals learning motivational interviewing methods (Miller, Yahne, Moyers, Martinez, & Pirritano, 2004), "mindfulness-based health coaching" (Spence, Cavanagh, & Grant, 2008), and feedback on "daily verbal safety communications with . . . workers" (Kines et al., 2010).

Absent a well-validated or at least consensually agreed-upon identification of coachable problems, research will not likely progress anytime soon. As important, consulting psychologists lack a basis for categorizing presenting issues and selecting an appropriate intervention. Of course, this is not to say that coaching cannot have more of an existential flair (e.g., Stelter, 2014) or simply be a sounding board, but even those somewhat ethereal goals can be translated into specific foci of coaching, such as "increasing understanding and meaning of one's life" and "has a confidential sounding board with whom to discuss ideas and concerns."

I am skirting two major issues. One is whether coaching should be directed only to identifying and fixing problematic areas of one's work performance or whether it can also be directed as a primary goal to making the already high-performing performers better (see, e.g., Jones & Spooner, 2006). The second major issue is whether coaching approaches need to be matched with the type of problem or issue at hand or can be driven by the preferred approach of the psychologist.

As for the first matter, I have used both the words *issue* and *problem* in identifying the focus of coaching. In fact, either can be the focus of coaching whereas in those approaches to change that aim only to fix defects the possibility is ignored that clients may not be seeking help for a "problem" but rather to make an existing skill or strength even better. To make my logic explicit: Taxonomies in mental health are almost all problem focused (depression, anxiety, etc.) because it is persons with psychological dysfunction who are largely those who receive therapy or psychotherapeutic treatment. Certainly, "truth seekers," or persons who simply want to explore their psyches with "trusted advisors," visit therapists, but there is little evidence that they make up a large percentage of those receiving treatment. In contrast, one can accept, in principle, the belief that people may seek out coaching without having a particular issue or problem but instead would like to better understand themselves and have help thinking through options; these could arguably be goals to which coaching can be directed. The coaching psychologist is advised, one way or the other, to clearly understand the focus of the coaching, to have some idea as to whether evidence indicates that coaching will positively address these issues, and to consider the possibility of alternative explanations for the reported behavior that need addressing by some other intervention approach (e.g., work problems secondary to primary depression; first, treat the depression; see Lowman, 1993a).

Sorting out the focus of the coaching should be given the time it deserves. Assessment, even without the use of psychological tests, can be directed not just to understanding the diagnostic category in which the presenting issues fall but also to identifying how the client conceptualizes these issues, the degree of discomfort associated with them, the client's motivation to work toward improvement, what solutions have been tried, the sticking points of bringing about change, and the general conceptual models with which the client is comfortable and familiar.

If, for example, a coaching client is describing a problem with procrastination at work (see, e.g., Konnikova, 2014; Sims, 2014; Surowiecki, 2010), the coach needs to identify whether this is a chronic or a narrowly focused problem; whether the client is capable of doing the work to the desired result; the consequences (to the workplace and to oneself) of delaying action; the positive gains of procrastination; the extent to which only work or other aspects of life are affected that the desired or anticipated behavior change; whether it is a long-standing and deeply seated problem or something more recent and circumscribed; and in the minds of the client and/or the coach, how urgently change is needed. The answers to those questions and the coach's conceptualization of the problem help the coaching psychologist determine a particular approach that is more likely to have a positive impact. For a narrowly defined focal issue, such as procrastinating on aspects of the job the client does not want to do, a simple behavioral approach (e.g., Duhigg, 2013) may be sufficient. When the evidence suggests a seriously dysfunctional pattern deriving from low self-esteem or low sense of self-efficacy, alternative approaches may be needed. Or when procrastination is really just a normal part of the work process (e.g., the need for ideas to gestate in creativity; Amabile, Barsade, Mueller, & Staw, 2005), the client may simply need a better understanding of this being a typical part of the work process that needs to be nurtured and protected.

The following case illustrates the complexity of the coaching process even when the focal concern is seemingly circumscribed.

Case 5: "I Keep Putting It Off"

Jon was 32 years old at the time he pursued coaching for help with what he defined as a problem with procrastination. In his annual review, he was criticized by his supervisor for too often turning reports in late or at the very last minute—including his self-evaluation for his annual review.

Jon usually did very high-quality work, but he drove his associates mad with his lateness in getting his part of projects to his team members and subordinates. In discussing with his psychologist coach whether this was a pattern and whether it was something in his personal life or just in his work life, it quickly became clear it was part of a long-standing pattern that affected most spheres of his life. In fact, it dated back to his school days when he worried incessantly about the adequacy of his work and hungered for the best possible grades. For the psychologist, the question was what was driving this dynamic, and a pattern of obsessional anxiety was identified. After a short period of cognitive behavioral coaching (Palmore & Williams, 2013; Peltier, 2009; Sherin & Caiger, 2004) in which little progress was made, the psychologist referred Jon to a psychologist specializing in anxiety disorders for further assessment.

Approaches to Coaching Versus Validated Interventions

Clearly, coaching is a field in the making, not one that is yet well-established from the perspective of science and validation. Consulting psychologists need, as any psychologist would, to apply in their work current knowledge and to be respectful of what is not known (see Lowman, 2013a). What does this mean? Currently, coaching is driven more by approaches than it is by a well-established and consensually agreed-upon taxonomy of types of issues. To argue, for example, that a particular approach to coaching (e.g., mindfulness; e.g., Cavanagh & Spence, 2013) works for a broad range of problems must be consistent with evidence that simply does not yet exist. (To their credit, Cavanagh & Spence's 2013 chapter, "Mindfulness in Coaching: Philosophy, Psychology or Just a Useful Skill?", presents a question that should be asked of most "approaches" to coaching.)

Coaching will only advance as a well-validated intervention as the literature advances, especially with well-designed studies executed by those who have no vested interest in the outcomes and who approach the research objectively. In the meantime, consulting psychologists who make use of coaching approaches need to make use of the empirical literature generated thus far, the larger case study literature, and training by those who have extensive experience working in this area who can contribute to their clinical knowledge. As psychologists, they are well advised to proceed with appropriate caution, to identify rule-out criteria in which some other form of intervention may be needed (see, e.g., Kaiser, LeBreton, & Hogan, 2015), and to evaluate the effectiveness of their efforts (see, e.g., Winum, Nielsen, & Bradford, 2002). Contributing, at the least, case studies to the literature will also, over time, build up the literature from which valid generalizations about coaching's efficacy can proceed.

OTHER INTERVENTION APPROACHES

Coaching remains the favored child when it comes to individual-level interventions, and a consulting psychologist can potentially find well-identified markets in which to apply coaching skills. Consulting psychologists have other types of skills that are also relevant for intervention. In this section I, identify some of them.

Career Counseling

Career assessment was discussed earlier in this chapter, but assessment may not be sufficient to sustain change over time. Career counseling (see, e.g., Hartung, Savickas, & Walsh, 2015; McIlveen, 2015; Savickas, 2011) relates to helping individuals understand their patterns and issues and to make or correct appropriate choices or decisions about possibilities that have become complicated. When people have chosen what arguably is a wrong career direction for them, have been in that career for some time, and then need to make a course correction, it can be far more complex than when one is still in college at the beginning of one's career. The difficult issue is to sort out the extent to which the career issue is subordinate to issues of psychopathology or vice versa.

Case 6: Physician, Heal Thyself?

Despite years of professional training and preparation Mark, a urologist, was finally coming to the realization he was quite unhappy in his day-to-day work. He was very gifted in science and memorized facts easily, so he had great facility with the symptoms and differentiating characteristics of various types of illness. Like many of his colleagues, he was fairly quiet and introverted, somewhat easy to anger when his views were questioned, and highly respected by his colleagues and patients alike. Mark had had many years of clinical training in hospitals but never had questioned his basic fitness for his career. His personal life was stable, if not very exciting to him, but increasingly he had to work harder and harder to experience pleasure in going to work. He had visited a psychiatrist when feeling particularly low and had been put on antidepressant medications. Mark's work had barely been mentioned when the decision was made to prescribe antidepressants, but his personal life (which Mark did not view as problematic) had been queried in detail from relationships to his interest in sex. The psychiatrist had defined the depression as primary and the work-related symptoms, to the extent the psychiatrist was aware of them, as derivative. Although over time Mark's mood lifted somewhat from the medication, he remained vaguely dissatisfied with his work, committed to doing a good job because he would never do less than that, but he was enjoying it less and less. Finally, he self-referred to a consulting psychologist specializing in career assessment and work-related counseling at the individual level.

The consulting psychologist met with Mark and suggested completion of a career assessment process, which in this case included assessment of psychopathology, as well as measures of normal personality, abilities, and interests. The psychologist spoke with Mark at some length and tried to differentiate what it was about his position that was unfulfilling. Was it really the career choice that was causing him unhappiness? Was he in the right career but not in the right place to practice it? Was he in the wrong area of specialization but well suited to medicine? Had something in his personal life spilled over into his professional life and was masking as a work problem?

Through the assessment process, it became clear to the psychologist that Mark, although enjoying the scientific and intellectual challenge of his work, the hard work, and the opportunities for self-reliance, did not really enjoy working with sick people. Was there some area or set of activities in medicine—a different medical specialty, perhaps—which might be better fitting? Although his occupational interest pattern (Holland, 1997; Lowman & Carson, 2012) of investigative–social–artistic was a good enough fit for Mark's career, the interests could find expression in other ways. The absence of realistic ("hands on") interests in his profile may have suggested a better fit with a helping occupation that was less hands on. Other areas of medical specialization might be suggested (psychiatry, for example; see O*NET, n.d.-d). But his pattern of abilities also identified a strong interest in creative work consistent with his artistic occupational interest pattern.

Mark concluded, with the input of his consulting psychologist, that it was time to consider changes in direction from his current niche in medicine. On the basis of the overall profile, including the interest–ability–personality profile (Lowman, 1991, 1993b; Lowman & Ng, 2010), a different specialization should be considered in medicine and/or different roles (e.g., teaching, research) within the field. The psychologist provided Mark information on some possible career directions for further exploration and met with him every few weeks for several months as he mulled over his options. Ultimately, Mark decided to build on his current career of medicine rather than make a radical change, but he sought out teaching and research roles and, in time, switched areas of specialization and primary job duties. With those changes, Mark's depression abated and stayed that way and he was again excited and again felt joy in his work.

Extensive evidence provided by Hogan, Kaiser, and colleagues (e.g., R. Hogan, 2006; Kaiser, Hogan, & Craig, 2008; and Kaiser, LeBreton, & Hogan, 2015) identifies the so-called dark side of leaders' personalities (which often seem to clearly overlap with personality disorders), another type of problem for which psychologists' assessment and intervention skills are relevant. Although such problematic patterns may result in the derailment of managers (see, e.g., J. Hogan, Hogan, & Kaiser, 2011), they may also leave a wake of problems and unhappiness in the organization. The extent to which such problems can be addressed effectively with counseling methods is unclear. Ensuring compliance with company rules, ethics, and expectations may be an appropriate purpose of coaching or counseling with such individuals, who, left to their own devices, may be destructive over the long term both to subordinates and peers and to the organization itself. For some "dark side" leaders coaching will not be effective and the coaching may need to be with organizational officials about the risks and need to manage assertively high risk strategies of such individuals.

Case 7: A Narcissistic Physician

Victoria came to the consulting psychologist for assistance with her work and personal life. Her marriage of 7 years was breaking up and she had received feedback from her supervisor at work, the chair of her hospital department, that she was not relating well to members of her team and that some patients had complained about her bedside manner (i.e., that she did not seem very empathic). At the suggestion (implied mandate) of her supervisor, she booked an appointment with a consulting psychologist specialist, who was located in a larger city several hours away from her small-city location. She arrived late for her appointment and was dressed a bit flamboyantly. In the psychologist's office, her presence quickly filled the room. The psychologist was sensitive to his own feelings and reactions (see Alderfer, 1968, 2011; Levinson, 2002b), and felt that the client had little understanding of how she was viewed by others on her team. The psychologist felt squeezed out of her own office by Victoria. Everything about Victoria's presentation suggested issues associated with a narcissistic personality (Lubit, 2002; Maccoby, 2004) yet she was highly competent in the technical aspects of her work roles over many years, and her job was not on the line. The psychologist concluded that her make-up was closer to "dark side" personality characteristics than to a full-blown personality disorder.

When the psychologist asked how she thought she was coming across in the meeting, Victoria responded positively, indicating that it was great finally for her to be meeting with a kindred spirit. In fact, the psychologist did not feel very connected to her client, much less like a kindred spirit, and felt somewhat suffocated, with no air in the room to breathe, and that, whatever her occupational achievements, this woman would be a difficult one with whom to work or with whom to be in a relationship. As always, the psychologist looked for the sometimes-small pocket of engagement where she could relate positively to the client and find common ground that would be the basis for a therapeutic relationship.

Recognizing the potential for narcissistic injury (Halewood & Tribe, 2003; Miller, 1981) before the client's defenses were able to handle what would likely be seen as severe criticism, the psychologist responded that her style in the meeting room came across as somewhat one-sided and

that, although she found Victoria engaging, personally she was having difficulty with the way that the two of them were relating, that it did not feel
very genuine or mutual. Victoria seemed surprised, but her attention had
been captured and she asked, a little too insistently, "What do you mean?"

Individual assessment identified a number of personality issues with
the client's profile. The psychologist, concluding that major personality
change was unlikely, worked with Victoria in coaching to increase her
understanding of how others were perceiving her. She continued to share
with her, at first gently, her own reactions to the client and wondered aloud
if others might have a similar reaction when interacting with her. She also
wondered, with Victoria, what might be driving this pattern—what were
her intentions in relating to others? This had some effect on Victoria's
subsequent behavior, and over time, the coaching sessions resulted in the
client's becoming more sensitive to the reactions of others and somewhat
more empathic.

Onboarding, Retirement, and Unemployment Coaching

Major life transitions often involve changes in the work role. Transitioning to the workplace and, ultimately, transitioning out of it may proceed
smoothly or not. For those not able to make the transition successfully on
their own, consulting psychologists can be helpful in addressing the psychological issues associated with retirement (Hansen, 2013; Sandhu, 2002),
unemployment (Englert, Sommerville, & Guenole, 2009; Pryor & Ward,
1985), and onboarding (Korte & Lin, 2013) transitions.

Case 8: Preretirement Coaching and Counseling

Jerold was 58 at the time of his referral for preretirement counseling. A
college professor in the humanities, he had planned to work at least until
age 65 and, with good health, until 70. However, his health had become
increasingly challenging, and he was experiencing some minor memory
lapses following a mild stroke that had occurred a year ago. Additionally,
most of his research was funded from external grants, and the funding
in his particular area of research had dried up, with decreasing prospects

of being able to sustain his salary support requirements expected in his university. The client had primarily been invested in his professional life throughout his career. Although he worked long hours they did not seem particularly long to him since he enjoyed his work. A bright, articulate, man who looked older than his stated age, Jerold expressed considerable unhappiness about the prospect of needing to retire. Because Jerold had very little experience in avocational activities, the consulting psychologist worked with him to acknowledge and begin to grieve the loss, to consider alternative outlets for his skill set, and to understand the ways in which his health problems were contributing to his sense of unease. Through a short course of coaching, Jerold began to let go of the overcontrolling tendencies that had characterized him throughout his career and to recognize that he would have to make substantial changes in his preferred life course but that there were still enjoyable activities for him. After having to retire from his university position, he became a volunteer in the extracurricular programs in his local K–12 school system. His health spiraled downward rapidly after an unexpected diagnosis of early Alzheimer's was made, and his volunteer activities had to stop. However, he had enriched his relationship with his spouse and children, who engaged with him with considerable intensity to support him in this difficult period.

SUMMARY

At the individual level, consulting psychologists can work to help make strong performers more effective, to help employers make better selection decisions, to help people experiencing work problems resolve them, and to help people with major life transitions into and out of their work roles. Although psychological methods appropriate for individual-level work are often used, coaching is not psychotherapy, and individual assessment is not usually used to identify psychopathology or to confirm a diagnosis. Rather, the goal is to improve human effectiveness and to assist people in the development of their core abilities and strengths.

3

Consulting at the Group and Team Level

Groups—also known in the consulting context as teams or work groups—are one of the fundamental units of an organization, and therefore consulting psychologists need to know about them, even though much of psychology research and of consulting psychology's literature often focuses primarily on the individual. Yet, in a world now highly interrelated and with a rapidly expanding knowledge base, work done primarily at the individual level is becoming less common. Of course, there are still people who work alone (e.g., those writing fiction or computer code), but even they are dependent on others for their work to reach beyond themselves.

Homans (1950) defined *groups* more generally:

> We mean by *group* a number of persons who communicate with one another often over a span of time, and who are few enough so that each person is able to communicate with all the others, not at secondhand, through other people, but face to face. (p. 1)

http://dx.doi.org/10.1037/14853-003
An Introduction to Consulting Psychology: Working With Individuals, Groups, and Organizations, by R. L. Lowman

It has been 65 years since Homans's (1950) classic *The Human Group* was published. Today one might tweak the definition of groups shown above to include, for example, more than "communication" as the defining tasks of groups. But Homans's book remains a classic, highly accessible, and well-written introduction to the nature and functions of groups, and it examines commonalities among groups as diverse as those in the Trobriand Islands in Papua New Guinea, the Bank Wiring Room of the Hawthorne Electric facility, a street gang, and an electrical equipment company.

Other definitions of *group* have also been offered. By the 1970s, Marvin Shaw (1971), for example, a major researcher in this area, defined a *group* as being "two or more persons who are interacting with one another in such a manner that each person influences and is influenced by each other person" (p. 10). Today, this definition can be extended to acknowledge explicitly that groups do not have to be in face-to-face communication or interaction with one another to constitute a group. But the basic ideas included in these definitions have not changed. *Groups* are social entities in which people interact with one another in a way that involves influence and that—for better or worse—can change individual-level behavior. (*Teams* is the term used to refer to a particular type of group, one found in work organizations in which the purpose of the group is to perform a coherent part of the purpose for which the organization exists in a bounded and interrelated collection of people.)

Despite some neglect by consulting psychology, groups have been studied for a long time (see Alderfer, 1968), particularly by social psychologists. Some of the most interesting early work was done in the context of the use of groups to change individual-level attitudes and behavior, demonstrating the potential to use group modalities to change individuals. During World War II, for example, Kurt Lewin (1948) and his colleague Alex Bavelas examined how the attitudes and behaviors of housewives toward the use of less desirable foods like intestinal meats (at a time of meat shortages and rationing) could be changed by group discussion versus simply providing information in lectures. The group discussion method was over 10 times more effective in behavioral change. They later replicated the study to examine whether groups were more effective than other methods in getting housewives to use evaporated rather than whole milk, another food item in short supply during the war. Similarly, Lewin and his colleagues found that the aspirational level of a group was affected by group discussion (Lewin, 1946). Lewin and colleagues' work on groups sparked an era of research into groups (see, e.g., Leonard & Freedman, 2000; Shaw, 1971).

The study of groups by psychologists did not begin in World War II, however. Some classic studies of work groups occurred even earlier than the influential wartime efforts. One of the most important of the early studies on groups in organizations (one that incidentally resulted in the identification of the eponymous "Hawthorne effect") was conducted at the Hawthorne Electric Works in Chicago in the 1920s and 1930s (see Homans, 1950; Roethlisberger & Dickson, 1939). A number of research studies but also interventions (including the little-remembered introduction of one of the first employee personal counseling programs; Dickson & Roethlisberger, 1966) were undertaken in this innovative work. But some of the most important findings of the research aspects of this study concerned the role and importance of work groups (teams) in influencing employee productivity, attitudes, understanding of what is expected and allowed, and embracing or opposing of change initiatives.

Other important milestones in group research and applications include the development of the National Training Laboratories (NTL; Freedman, 1999), whose approach was using unstructured groups with team facilitators through which members could learn about their behavior in small groups in which the usual behavioral expectations were absent. A related approach that focused more on reactions individuals had to strict boundaries and the exercise of power in groups was the Tavistock approach (see Gould, Stapley, & Stein, 2004; Hugg, Carson, & Lipgar, 1993). As these modalities were applied to work groups their uses, but also their limitations, were increasingly noted. T-groups, for instance, as sensitivity training programs came to be called, had their share of psychological casualties, especially with poor facilitators and those participants who were psychologically fragile before the group began (Hartley, Roback, & Abramowitz, 1976).

COMPONENTS, STRUCTURE, AND PROCESSES OF GROUPS AND TEAMS

When employees come to work they bring with them their own collection of knowledge, skills, abilities, and personality, but they apply them in the context of a specific organization, their employer. The organizational employer may be successful or struggling and may emphasize innovation or stasis. It may pay well, average, or poorly compared with other employment opportunities but its culture is likely to be influential. Still, that is only part of what shapes employees behavior. On a day-to-day basis, interactions in work groups are likely to occur in the context of a specific collection of people who interact regularly, directly, and predictably.

Here I review some of the basic properties of groups and consider why groups matter to consulting psychologists and why they are ignored, as has often been the case in study, at the psychologist's peril. (As one example of that consider that most of the extensive literature on personnel selection addresses primarily individual characteristics of people in the context of individual-level outcomes; see, e.g., Mohammed, Cannon-Bowers, & Foo, 2010.) Groups matter greatly in organizations because they are the level at which much of the work gets done. Indeed, in modern complex organizations, there is rather little work that does not involve interaction among individuals and also between groups.

Developmental History and "Working Parts" of Groups and Teams

Groups may take their origins from accidental geographic juxtapositions of individuals in classrooms, from marriage and procreation, from assignment to a formal team as part of defined work roles, or by voluntary associations of friends whose primary purpose in being together is the fulfillment of social needs. What makes assemblies of people into groups (as Homans, 1950, included in his definition and Shaw, 1971, elaborated) is their interdependence on each other, their having regular contact and interaction with one another, and their purpose.

Over time, collections of individuals who are in some way engaged with and interdependent on one another evolve. The group assumes not only an identity of its own with boundaries of who is and who is not in the group, it usually also has a name. This applies both to teams and work groups and others as well. Families, e.g., are groups, have a function and purpose, and a name that helps to communicate who is in or out of the group. Boundaries identify those who are in the group and those who are excluded. As members work together, groups also develop *norms*, that is, behavioral expectations and characteristic ways of interacting with one another. People who meet or exceed normative expectations can be rewarded, and those who underperform ("slackers") or who seriously violate the norms may be sanctioned or forced to leave the group. Group members bring with them prior personal identities, but the group membership itself can become part of its members' individual identities (e.g., I am an engineer; a member of a family; the leader of, e.g., the Design or Research and Development Team; a supervisor).

In this section are summarized some of the basic defining elements of work groups that may be important to consider in consultation work at the group level.

Group Formation

Groups in organizations can be long-standing or of more recent creation. They may be intentionally and formally established or develop organically or informally. Groups that have existed long past the tenure of the current group incumbents are more likely to be more stable and to have well-established work processes to which newer group members must adapt. New groups have less cultural baggage and therefore may be more amenable to change.

Some foundational questions to consider asking when consulting with work groups include:

- When did this group/team get started?
- How long have the present members of the group/team been working together?

- Have the members of this group/team changed much over time?
- How easy is it for new members of the group/team to get fully acclimated?
- As you think about members of the group/team no longer with it, what caused them to leave?

Type of Group and Purpose or Task

The purpose of the team or group will influence who joins. Groups of scientists or groups with technical purposes will likely attract bright introverts who are more comfortable with ideas or things than with people. Conversely, social groups and those in helping organizations are likely to attract sociable people who enjoy interacting with people.

Groups can also be formal ones, as in work groups set up by an organization to perform the tasks and duties of various jobs. Or, they can be informal ones that develop from friendships or allegiances that may cut across formal group boundaries. Employees are likely to be part of more than one group, and the intersections of these groups may foster alignment or contribute to group conflict.

Questions to consider asking about the type of group derive from its purpose:

- What are the major purposes of this group/team?
- Have those purposes changed over time?
- Who decides to change the team's purposes or major functions?
- Would you say that this group/team exists mostly for work-related or for social purposes or for some combination?

Group Composition

This variable addresses the question of who is in or is not part of the group. In work organizations, groups are composed of individuals whose talents are thought collectively to be needed to get a job done. In the context of employee selection, considerable research (Forsyth, 2009; see, e.g., Seong, Kristof-Brown, Park, Hong, & Shin, 2015; Shaw, 1971) has been done to date on how a group's abilities can be summative of the individuals' abilities. More recently, personality variables have been considered in the context of group composition. This research includes consideration of whether personality interacts with abilities in group contexts, as is the case when predicting to performance at the individual level. Also interesting is the possibility that certain individuals are not likely to thrive in groups (Barry & Stewart, 1997; Walker, 2007).

Freedman and Leonard (2002) noted the following paradoxes with respect to team membership:

> Diversity and individuality are prized in assembling teams and then all team members are expected to pull together as if there were no significant differences in team members' interests, loyalties, goals, values, outlooks, or personality makeups. . . . Each team member must come to terms with the inescapable tension created by the dilemma of simultaneously feeling the desire to behave as an individual while at the same time recognizing the need to suppress their individuality . . . in order to coalesce into a cohesive . . . team. (p. 33)

Yet, Hackman (2002) noted that work groups most likely to have "great performances" were likely to be larger (with more heterogeneity of talents in the group).

Questions to consider asking about group membership include:

- Are there more men or women in this group?
- How diverse is the ethnic make-up of the group/team?
- How does the group handle "differentness"?
- How are minorities in the group treated?
- How do group members perceive themselves as being treated?
- In what ways are group members expected to conform and suppress their individuality as part of being a group member?

Boundaries

Boundaries are demarcations of criteria for membership in a group that help to identify who is in and who is not part of the group. They can be formalized as in job descriptions or organizational charts. Alternatively, boundaries may be permeable to varying degrees, such that they can be more rigid or more flexible and may vary as to ease of entry (Morrison, Fast, & Ybarra, 2009). Boundaries can also be physical, time dependent, behavioral, or influenced by process (Freedman & Leonard, 2002).

Questions to consider asking about boundaries include:

- How do you tell who is part of the group/team and who is not?
- How receptive are members of this group/team to those outside the group/team?
- What happens when members of the group/team either leave on their own or by request?

Norms

Norms can be both formal and informal rules that are communicated directly and/or indirectly to new members of the group. Often, new employees learn by hearing or reading the formal rules and by observing others (or experiencing their sanctions) to learn what the informal rules are. As Homans (1950) observed,

> The rule of the Bank Wiremen that no one should wire much more or less than two equipments [sic] a day was a true norm, because . . . the social standing of a member of the group declined as he departed in one way or another form the norm. Nonconformity was punished and conformity rewarded. (p. 123)

Norms also relate to the range of behavior that individuals are permitted to show in the workplace. As Thompson (1967) noted,

> The inducements/contributions contract sets limits to the behavior that the individual is to exhibit in the organizational context, therefore reducing the heterogeneity of humans. . . . The contract, explicitly or by implication, also provides limits on the organization; it can call on a limited array of the individual's total repertoire of possible behavior. (pp. 105–106)

Questions to consider asking about norms include:

- What are some of the "rules of the road" for this group/team?
- What expectations does the group/team have for its members?

- How does the group/team communicate to its members what is expected of them?
- Would you say that the organization or the group/team has more to say about behavioral expectations in the group?
- What happens to those who violate the group's/team's informal or formal rules?
- What kind of behavior is positively regarded and rewarded in the group/team?
- How easy is it to make changes to the unwritten or formal rules in this group?

Roles

Talents and personality of members of a work group differ, although occupations and to some extent organizations act as an invisible hand attracting well-suited individuals to particular types of work and repelling (or rejecting) individuals that do not have the interests–abilities–personality (see Lowman, 1991, 1993b). *Roles* can refer to work tasks that are reliably and predictably assigned to groups of employees or to psychological roles such as the process leader or task leaders of the group. Roles can be adaptive but can also be stultifying.

Questions to consider asking about group roles include:

- Of the various activities done by this group, who is assigned which tasks?
- Who would you say is or are most attentive to the social or process side of things?
- Are there formal and informal leaders in this group?
- How much variability in assigned or assumed roles is there in this group?
- Have the roles in the group varied over time? Do they change as new people enter the group?

Communication Patterns

Some of the most impactful aspects of a group have to do with how its members communicate with those in the group, and those outside the group, including between the organization's leadership and team members. Communication is both formal and informal.

When teams are virtual or otherwise not colocated, communication is more likely to be strained, insufficient, or absent. Language barriers may arise when members of a team are in different countries. Even teams whose members are located in the same physical building may seldom meet face-to-face and therefore fail to develop the intuitive understanding of the people with whom members are supposed to be working collaboratively.

Questions to consider asking about communication patterns include:

- Is most formal communication within the organization from top levels down or in both directions?
- What is the tone of formal communications? Are they more likely to be positive and upbeat, accentuating the commonalities or the differences among various constituencies in the organization?
- How is dissent handled in groups? Do those with contrary views get heard?
- Are there different leaders for different types of communication? Is humor initiated by many or just a few individuals in the group?
- How do people respond when different members communicate? Whose communications are taken more seriously and whose, less so?
- Do group communication patterns differ by minority status within the group?
- Are microaggressions against group members acknowledged?

Leadership

Groups can have formal leaders (often called "task leaders") or, in the case of social groups, no designated leader. One way or another, leaders tend to emerge in ongoing groups. In assessing leadership in groups consulting psychologists can consider the types of tasks needing to be accomplished by the group and for which leadership roles may emerge. Common leadership roles in groups or teams include task and emotional leadership (Beck, 1981). Freedman and Leonard (2002) also identified the "limits/assumption-testing leader," who brings to the attention of the group the suppression of individual differences and/or who questions others' assumptions, and the "commitment leader," who moderates the task focus of the team leader by focusing on the degree to which the goals are achievable.

Questions to consider asking in this area include:

- Who are the appointed (or formal) leaders in the group?
- Who are the informal leaders in the group?
- Who looks after the emotional needs of the group?
- Who in the group focuses primarily on getting the task done?
- Who challenges the assumptions in the group?
- Who questions assigned tasks when unrealistic goals have been set?
- Are people competing for leadership in the group? How are conflicts in leadership efforts addressed?
- How are the formal leaders of the group viewed by higher level managers?
- When leadership has changed how similar were the new leaders to the prior ones?

Developmental Issues

Groups have a history in time. They have a beginning, a middle, and ultimately, an end. Newly formed teams have different dynamics from ones whose members have been working together for long periods of time. New teams are more likely to have the excitement, optimism, and confusion associated with start-ups in general. Team members' beliefs and ways of doing things may become more fixed in work groups with greater longevity. They may therefore be less quick to change, and other groups or individuals outside the team may take for granted the team's preferred ways of doing things. Longer lived teams in organizations may also have seen a long litany of changes in the organization and about the latest organizational change initiative may have the attitude that "this too shall pass." Consultants should assess, if only briefly, the team's history, changes in leadership and membership over time, the team's successes and perceived failures, and how the norms, roles, and status have changed over time.

Questions to consider asking in this area include:

- How long has the group been in existence?
- Has its mission and purpose changed over time?

- Is the group more or less receptive to change now compared with in the past?
- What do group members regard as being their best and worst times?
- Is the group viewed as being flexible and productive by others in the environment?
- What are the group's aspirations (hopes, wishes, dreams), and are these mostly shared by everyone in the group?

Group Process Issues

Group process can be facilitative or disruptive of the tasks the team exists to serve. When people on the team enjoy working with other team members and care about the mission of the group and the larger organization in which it is embedded, groups enhance the performance of its individual members. When, inevitably, dysfunctional conflict among group members or between the group and other groups or people in the organization occurs, performance can be impeded. Persistent conflict or other process problems can cause chronic difficulty for the team or chronic under-performance. But conflict of ideas is inevitable and can be constructive, especially when not personalized.

Other group process issues include how people feel treated by others and by their leadership, which contributes to their sense of well-being and support. Similarly, the affect or emotions exhibited by the leader can contribute, by emotional contagion, to the group's sense of positive or negative emotions (S. K. Johnson, 2008).

Questions to consider asking to assess group processes include:

- What is the predominant affect observed in the group or team?
- When conflicts arise, how are they handled?
- How long do any residual effects of conflict last?
- What is the ratio of positive to negative affect in routine communications among group members?
- Do people in the group feel mostly supported and part of a cohesive team or unappreciated and mistreated?
- Do people feel that they can raise concerns with one another directly or is conflict suppressed and avoided?

Groups and the study of groups are complex, and other facets that can be studied and considered include group and organizational structure, performance, intergroup behavior, and group–organizational design issues. Studying groups, working with them, and helping organizations create groups in a way that makes best use of their desirable features is time well spent by consulting psychologists, in part because groups have a lot of potential to help an organization meet its goals.

LEARNING GROUP ASSESSMENT SKILLS

In graduate-level classes on organizational change and development, I require students to work in teams of two to jointly observe one ongoing work group on two separate occasions. They then write up their observations independently on the following factors:

1. *Describe the group.* Describe the nature, purpose, and constituency of the group.
2. *Is this a group?* Using the text and readings definitions of what constitutes a group (number of persons, interdependency, etc.), show how this is a group.
3. *Describe patterns of group interaction.* Who spoke to whom? Were patterns of interaction recurring (e.g., whenever X asserted, Y responded).
4. *Describe the roles in the group.* Describe how commonly occurring group roles (e.g., task leader, process leader) were executed by the group. What functional role did each person in the group play? Did the roles change over the course of your observation?
5. *How effective was the group?* Did the group accomplish its tasks? How efficiently? What sources of resistance were observed in the group? What did the group appear to do well and less well?
6. *What was the role of the observers?* How did the presence of the observers affect the group process? What were your own reactions to being in the observer roles? How did the dynamics of the interactions between the two of you affect the observational process? (Lowman, 2015)

After completing this portion of the assignment the two observers exchange their papers to learn their common perceptions and what the other team member observed that they missed and how two people each limited to observational roles can view the same process and see different things. I strongly recommend this simple exercise as a way for trainees to begin the process of learning the fundamentals of groups and to begin to feel comfortable in their presence.

It is common to use interview or face-to-face approaches in assessing smaller work groups. When the assessment is not of a single group but, e.g., of all the groups in an organization, survey methods (e.g., Church & Waclawski, 1998) are more commonly used.

Case 9: Assessing Individual and Team Dynamics in Virtual Groups

While still a graduate student in the consulting psychology doctoral program at Alliant International University in San Diego, Alex Howland (real name) and his colleagues then employed by the Rady School of Management at the University of California, San Diego, won a $1.7 million prize from the Graduate Management Admissions Council, the creators of the admissions test widely used by business schools for assessing candidates for admission to master's of business administration (MBA) programs. His proposal for this entrepreneurial competition was to create a virtual world by which business teams consisting of MBA students from major programs around the world were able to work together to solve business problems in a competitive environment. Working with artists, gamers, and content experts, he created VirBELA (http://www.virbela.com), a virtual world of MBA student teams from premiere graduate schools around the world. He and his collaborators tested the virtual team model, composed of cross-school MBA students (the members of each team could not be from the same school or country).

The monetary prizes for which the teams competed was a substantial motivator to participants, but as MBA students, they were competitive, enjoyed games with clear winners and losers, and played to win. Despite being in a virtual environment, being represented by avatars (although using their own voices), team dynamics varied substantially from one team to another, with less cohesion and more dysfunctionality shown by the teams competing less effectively. Here were groups of strangers, competing in teams with people they had never met in person, with broad differences in culture, but they might as well have been in the same room—their personality characteristics were evident, despite being thousands of geographic miles apart. The system proved to be an excellent medium for assessing both individual and group dynamics and the rich interactions among each.

GROUP-LEVEL INTERVENTIONS

Group interventions vary as to whether they are directed largely to individual behavior using the group as the change modality (as with sensitivity training, or Tavistock groups; T-groups) or to the groups themselves. In the latter case, groups have been the focus of systematic efforts that capitalize on their contributions to organizations (see D. A. Johnson, Beyerlein, Huff, Halfhill, & Ballentine, 2002), including the more recent initiative to apply coaching skills to groups (Hackman & Wageman, 2005). The late Richard Hackman's work (e.g., 1987, 1990, 2002; Hackman & Wageman, 2005) has been seminal in showing the importance of groups to organizations, their functions and dysfunctions, and in charting the way to an initial understanding of interventions. The important work of the Center for the Study of Work Teams (see, e.g., D. A. Johnson et al., 2002), for a number of years housed at the University of North Texas, has also made significant contributions to assessment and intervention of work groups in live organizational contexts. Alderfer's work (e.g., 1987, 1998) has also been significant in identifying the role and importance of identity groups (those based on personal characteristics such as race, age, gender) in organizational processes. And of course much of this important work stood on the shoulders of the giants in the field of psychology—including Kurt Lewin (1951), Solomon Asch (1951/1965), Phillip Zimbardo (e.g., Haney, Banks, & Zimbardo, 1973), Sherif and Sherif (1958), and Theodore Newcomb (1943)—who demonstrated early on the importance of groups as social psychological phenomena and as a vehicle for changing individual attitudes and behaviors (see Freedman, 1999; Freedman & Leonard, 2002; Leonard & Freedman, 2000;

Lewin, 1951). Leonard and Freedman (2000) noted that the focus in psychology in the second half of the 20th century, in contrast to the first half, has been on groups rather than individuals. As the concern with groups has developed to studying them in the context of work organizations, a number of intervention approaches have been developed. The theory for such interventions derives largely from the social psychology of small groups adapted for use in the work place.

Group-level interventions vary as to whether they are addressing dysfunction or are undertaken to improve the overall functioning of the organization, as with setting up new team structures within an existing organization. Small-group intervention with dysfunctional groups, such as those with overly rigid boundaries, those that are overly conflictual, or those with poor leader–team relationships, would often be undertaken on an ad hoc basis by consulting psychologists. The goal is to assess the problems, make recommendations, and in some cases, help implement the changes. Changes may include identifying new leadership for the team, facilitating conflict management activities, and conducting intergroup interventions to lessen the stress between groups.

An issue in all consulting interventions is whether the intent is to solve immediate problems for the short run or to design changes that are likely to prevail for the longer term. Building changes that last over time adds a complex challenge because, as with individual-level change, change for groups may not last.

D. A. Johnson et al. (2002) noted that in a National Science Foundation–supported study conducted in nine organizations, participants in group enhancement intervention projects experienced changes as frequently getting "worse before better," that the time needed to be invested is considerable (150–200 hours of formal training a year was typical of the more successful organizations' investment), and that affective reactions to change included fear, stress, and pain (see also Kozusznik, Rodríguez, & Peiró, 2015). Their findings argued for interventions conducted in an integrated rather than piecemeal manner and for changes that had the commitment of long-term support by those managing the changes. They also found that assessing the organization's climate and managing the stress associated with organizational change led to better outcomes (D. A. Johnson et al., 2002, pp. 253–255).

Of course, not all teams or work groups are created equally, nor do all confront the same types of issues. As described above, noncolocated work teams encounter issues about how to address group problems when members have often never met one another in person. Another aspect of groups, be they colocated or noncolocated, are the complex interactions of privilege, national origin/location, and subgroups (see Lopez & Ensari, 2013). Teams with issues related to members' identities (e.g., perceptions of disparate treatment associated with race, gender, or age) may need specialized types of intervention. Issues associated with the development of teams or groups also differ from those involved in consulting on dysfunction (Hackman & Wageman, 2005).

Certain process-oriented approaches may provide a theoretical basis that generalizes across situations. For example, Argyris (1971) introduced a model in his book *Intervention Theory and Method* that included the following three major functions of consulting:

1. creation of valid and useful information;
2. free and informed choice; and
3. internal commitment to choices made.

Using these three goals as an overarching framework for consulting clearly provides a meta-approach in which to anchor assessment and intervention activities, but any intervention or assessment also needs to be applied in the context of specific issues and groups/teams. Additionally, consulting psychologists need to determine the particular tools, frameworks, and research findings that are relevant to the particular coaching assignment.

GROUPS IN THE CONTEXT OF ORGANIZATIONS

Consulting psychologists may work with work groups in isolation from the rest of the organization, or they may work with them in the context of the larger organization. Social psychologists in the 1950s and beyond mostly examined groups as social psychological phenomena. Groups lent themselves well to laboratory studies in which various aspects of behavior could be controlled, such as in Asch's (1951/1965) and Zimbardo's (Haney et al., 1973) experiments or those of Lewin (1951). Such studies are particularly valuable in singling out aspects of behavior that occur under specified conditions and particularly with strangers who are assembled to be part of a group.

Groups implemented in organizations are much more complicated, both to research, design, and implement successfully and to provide consultation. Below, I present two types of group interventions that have proven successful in applications: participative work groups and groups associated with Scanlon Plan organizations.

Participative Work Groups

A highly successful approach to quality management that makes good use of the group in service of the organization is that of Edward Deming (1986). As an engineer, Deming advocated the need for total quality management but also emphasized the value of work groups in diffusing the quality focus. His approaches were largely ignored in the United States until after they became revered and widely adopted in Japan and after Japanese products became highly sought after. Deming's philosophy has 14 major points, including breaking down the divisions between management and workers, and creating a culture that includes groups of employees to which quality control is widely diffused. Quality circles and other participative approaches to quality control (see, e.g., Srinivasan & Kurey, 2014) have made heavy use of peer relationships and groups devoted to quality.

The Scanlon Plan

The Scanlon Plan (Frost, 1996; Frost, Wakeley, & Ruh, 1974; Moore & Ross, 1978; White, 1979) is an interesting labor–management cooperation approach to organization development that emerged out of the post–World War II labor unrest. The approach was centered, initially, at the MIT Labor Relations Department and later at Michigan State University.

The basic idea is that when management and labor cooperate around a common goal of improving cost–benefit ratios and a portion of the cost savings were shared with everyone (at all levels of the organization) the incentives to cooperate outweighed those to favor group-focused incentives. An essential part of the Scanlon Plan is a series of participative management committees in which employees are encouraged to identify cost savings ideas that would result in lower production costs. The groups' purposes are linked with organizational objectives but also provided an incentive for employees. Companies that have successfully adopted Scanlon Plans include Donnelly Mirrors, Herman Miller, Beth Israel Deaconess Medical Center, Firestone Tire and Rubber Company, and Motorola. Consulting psychologists working with such systems need to be able to work at the organizationwide as well as the group levels.

SUMMARY AND CONCLUSIONS

Groups or work teams can be powerful sources to achieve, or to impede, organizational goals. Groups have been studied by social psychologists and, more recently, by organizational psychologists. Following an earlier emphasis on individuals, concern with groups emerged with particular focus during and after World War II. Since then, work groups have been identified by a number of researchers and practitioners as being phenomena not to be ignored by consulting and organizational psychologists. The approaches that have been demonstrated to have the best outcomes in improving the performance and processes of teams and groups focus on organization-wide interventions, are supported by top management, address stressors associated with change, and recognize that the change process will often make things worse before they become better.

4

Consulting at the Organizational Level

Just as the evolution of life progressed from individual cells to simple organisms to complex multiple element systems, so too did work develop from lesser to greater complexity. Early on, work focused on individual or family-based simple survival tasks to work done in groups (e.g., hunting and fishing, agriculture, child rearing, domestic activities) to small organizations with multiple parts, to today's huge and highly complex multinational corporations. Psychologists have focused mostly on individuals (or small groups) and have less often studied or received supervised experience assessing or intervening with organizations. As a graduate student or junior professional, one does not typically have entire organizations as clients. At most, one may have responsibility for consulting to a small organization or be part of a team responsible for a consulting project with a small part of a larger organization.

It is not just that psychologists or psychologists in training have limited experience in consulting to entire organizations but also psychology

http://dx.doi.org/10.1037/14853-004
An Introduction to Consulting Psychology: Working With Individuals, Groups, and Organizations,
by R. L. Lowman

has few theories that have dealt with organizations as a whole. Economists, for example, examine data at the organizational level, but they primarily consider the financial aspects of organizations, whereas psychologists' areas of expertise is usually the people side of organizations.

Theories with more of a psychological base included March and Simon's (1958/1993) models, which built on then-existing organizational-level theories. These models of organizations were mostly framed at the individual level with some consideration of group influences, focusing especially on the work motivation of employees and their "decision" to participate, or not, in the organization in an engaged rather than superficial way.

This work critiqued existing theories of human behavior in the workplace that were based on models of rationality. Chapter 6, "Cognitive Limits on Rationality," of March and Simon's (1958/1993) *Organizations* was one of the earliest statements of Simon's theory of the cognitive limits of rationality, work for which he would later go on to win the Nobel Prize in economics. And indeed, this important early work was more influential for its critique of existing economic models of the behavior of humans in organizations than for its exposition of an overarching theory of organizational-level psychology.

One of the most influential works attempting to study organizations as a whole was the seminal work of Katz and Kahn (1966; revised in 1978) *The Social Psychology of Organizations.* This book introduced systems theory as a way of considering organizations as a whole, and it was noteworthy for not only organizing the extant research findings but also for the "systems" metaphor, which has had widespread utility. Katz and Kahn articulated an approach that viewed organizations as living systems that must closely exist within an environment, as having subsystems that get the work of the organization done, and as having multiple paths through which organizations can achieve their goals. The trouble with the model was (and is) that by the time the second (and last) edition of this classic work came out, it had become clear that many of the specific topics in the book had to be studied in their own right and had an ever-expanding literature of their own.

Another influential early book was Thompson's (1967) *Organizations in Action.* This work struggled with the inevitable quandary about which levels (e.g., individuals vs. organizations) upon which to focus. Thompson provided a series of propositions (e.g., "Proposition 7.8: When knowledge of cause/effect relationships is known to be incomplete, organizations under rationality norms evaluate component units in terms of organizational (rather than technical) rationality"; p. 95).The book began to identify the individual–group–organization dynamic by raising issues of organizational power, coalitions, dispersed versus aggregated power, and discretionary positions (i.e., those whose incumbents have the power to make decisions).

The same year Thompson's book was published, another important work, Rensis Likert's (1967) *The Human Organization: Its Management and Value*, appeared. At the time Likert[1] (widely known for the eponymous Likert scale) was the founding director of the Institute for Social Research (ISR) at the University of Michigan.[2] ISR was founded in 1949 and is funded almost entirely by grants and contracts. ISR's reliance on external funding forced it to grapple with major issues of the day rather than esoteric research questions of little practical importance. Likert's 1967 book and model derived from his earlier work, *New Patterns of Management* (1961). Although clearly based on empirical research, his models of management were in many ways prescriptive, arguing for the value of participative management in an era when the norm was more autocratic management. Perhaps for these reasons his models found a wide and appreciative audience.

In his approach to organizational leadership Likert (1967) posited four managerial "systems of organization," ranging from "exploitative authoritative" to "participative." It is perhaps not surprising that the participative models had better outcomes than did the more "authoritative" ones since ISR, where the model was developed, espoused such values. Likert (1967) also identified a number of approaches that crossed the line between the "people" and the "business" (or administrative) sides of organizations: human asset accounting, models for achieving effective coordination, group decision making, high performance goals, and models of institutional change.

---

[1] The name *Likert* is too often mispronounced (i.e., the *i* is short and not long).

[2] My first professional job after graduate school was at ISR and the Department of Psychology at the University of Michigan.

In the same era, an influential and rather remarkable book, Karl Weick's (1979) *The Social Psychology of Organizing* (original edition, 1969), also appeared and reframed many issues, starting with the book's title, which includes the word *organizing* rather than *organizations*. Weick, rather obscurely, defined *organizing* as "a consensually validated grammar for reducing equivocality by means of sensible interlocked behaviors" (p. 3). In many ways suggestive of the influential book by Watzlawick, Weakland, and Fisch (1974), *Change: Principles of Problem Formation and Problem Resolution*, Weick provides provocative illustrations of his major points. As a prototypical example:

> *The* basic theme for the entire organizing model is found in the following recipe for sense-making: "How can I know what I think until I see what I say?" Organizations are presumed to talk to themselves over and over to find out what they're thinking. That's basically what this entire book is about. . . . The organism or group enacts equivocal raw talk, the talk is viewed retrospectively, sense is made of it, and this sense is then stored as knowledge in the retention process. The aim of each process has been to reduce equivocality and to get some idea of what has occurred. (Weick, 1979, pp. 133–134)

In other words, organizations are not static entities, stable and predictable over time. Nor do models of "rationality" of individual organizational players address how organizations behave. Rather, the organization is viewed as being an "output" rather than an input, such that organizations (presumably, people within them) act first and make sense later, working backward to a theory of action. The interpretation of the enacted environment then becomes the source of subsequent actions and interpretations. Weick's conceptualizing also suggested that an organization's interpretation of the environment needs to consider the ways in which the organization itself has acted have caused the environment to be as it is.

Clearly, prescriptive theories are easier to apply to action than are research-oriented theories of organizational behavior. Such approaches reduce complexity and help the psychologist identify what is thought to be wrong with an organization and how interventions will be made. However, the broader point is that it is difficult to theorize and to conduct empirical research about work organizations as a whole that translates into action. At best, psychologists are usually working with a small number of the organization's moving parts and necessarily are ignoring many other functions, parts, or processes. (The same might be said of treatment of ailments of the human body, with far fewer moving parts than the typical complex organization.)

Even consulting psychologists who do not start with a prescriptive approach inevitably will have to act to reduce the complexity when they interact with "live" organizations. They may do this in different ways, some more acceptable than others. Some consultants, for example, essentially espouse one approach or theory that they then try to apply to a variety of situations. At times, the fit is good and the theories of choice and the consulting actions work well. In other situations, the fit is not good, and it is only the persuasiveness of the consultant that allows the work to continue and (by some at least) to be regarded as worth doing.

Even more than with groups, organizations benefit from what might be called mini theories that help to explain in detail defined parts of the organization or to address specific problems affecting the organization. Organizational psychology has few, if any, "grand theories" that successfully explain everything about an organization relevant to a particular type of issue of problem. Nor are psychologists usually trained or equipped to diagnose or intervene in many aspects of organizations that are of potential relevance to the problems with which an organization is trying to deal. Understanding at least the basic aspects of the larger system while working with the concrete problems the organization is experiencing and for which it seeks help provides greater perspective and less likelihood of doing harm. For example, one might ask: What is the state of the economy in general? Are most organizations experiencing financial difficulty and having to cope with layoffs or terminations of employees? What is the state of the particular industry in which the organization competes? Is it new and emerging or highly competitive? What is the state of the supply and demand for jobs in this particular industry? Is it a buyer's or a seller's market for talent? What competitive strategies appear to be working in the marketplace? Is the particular organization with which the consultant is working a major player in its competitive marketplace? Is it gaining or losing market share? Is the organization in trouble or generally functioning well overall? Is it meeting its performance objectives?

Psychologists do not have to be economists, accountants, experts in manufacturing, or marketing to be helpful to organizations. But they do need to know their limits and be prepared to work with professionals with expertise other than their own to serve the needs of their client. And they need to learn enough about their clients' industries, competitive and economic pressures, and the state of the micro- and macroeconomies in which they are involved to know what the overall pressures are with which the organization as a whole are dealing.

ASSESSMENT

To some extent, the types of assessment of organizations that psychologists undertake will be driven by their theories of organizations and their theories and understanding of the particular parts of the organization with which they are dealing (see, e.g., Howard, 1994). The few efforts to date to provide systemic approaches to diagnosing and intervening with organizations as a whole have not been without problems. I discuss some of these approaches below.

Levinson's Approach

One of the earlier approaches to organizational diagnosis was that of Harry Levinson, who trained as a clinical psychologist but worked as a consulting psychologist. His approach to organizational assessment was intended to be comprehensive and mirrored clinical approaches at the individual level (Levinson, 1972, 2002a, 2002b, 2002c). Levinson began his career working with the Topeka State Hospital, which was a seriously flawed organization in which patients were poorly treated in antiquated facilities (see Sashkin, 1982). His study and interests led to major reforms and improvement. His training had been as a clinical psychologist at the University of Kansas and the Menninger Foundation. Subsequently, he taught organizational diagnosis and consulting at Harvard University's

Business School and later its medical school. Through his own consulting firm, The Levinson Institute, he consulted for many major business and governmental organizations.

Levinson wrote widely on organizational consultation issues, often anchoring his writings in his experiences as a consulting psychologist. The first comprehensive overview of his organizational diagnostic model appeared in the widely read book *Organizational Diagnosis* (Levinson, 1972). A second version of the volume was published 30 years later (Levinson, 2002b), with the title *Organizational Assessment: A Step-by-Step Guide to Effective Consulting*. He also was expert at making psychological concepts accessible to managers (see Lowman, Diamond, & Kilburg, 2012).

Levinson's approach to organizational diagnosis rested on several assumptions, including (a) the organization's history was important in understanding its present; (b) managers, employees, and in turn, organizations are motivated by both conscious and unconscious processes; (c) how the consultant was treated by those in the organization was often indicative of problems or issues in the organization; and (d) consultants' own feelings and reactions (countertransference) provided important information about the organization and the people within it suggesting the consultant's own self as a diagnostic instrument (Levinson, 1972, 2002a, 2002b, 2002c). Illustrating several of these points, Levinson (in a 2002 interview; as cited in Diamond, 2003) said:

> Without the concept of unconscious processes, consultants work at a manifest and superficial level of structure and strategy without understanding the psychological meaning of these perpetuated structures and strategies and thereby without a lens for interpreting irrational and dysfunctional practices. The framework for organizational diagnosis was intended to provide analysts and consultants a method for studying manifest and latent organizational dynamics by combining factual, genetic, and historical data with crucial interpretive [or narrative] data. More importantly, it enables consultants to root their articulation of organizational problems in a consensually validated narrative. (p. 8)

Levinson was not dogmatic about his particular approach to organizational diagnosis versus alternative diagnostic models, and his approach in practice seemed to be focused on the phenomena at hand. He articulated this idea well in the following:

> Psychoanalytic organizational consultancy, unlike most consultancy practices, requires a stance of open mindedness, an acknowledgement of "not knowing" and thereby a suspension of the assumption of knowing. This humility is derived from self-knowledge. My concern with the theory and practice of organizational diagnosis today is that some organizational analysts and consultants, particularly those who claim to assume a psychoanalytic orientation, are not sufficiently equipped with adequate insights into their own defensive proclivities and are thereby incapable of differentiating between their private world of internal object relations and that of their clients and their client systems. In other words, unanalysed or unacknowledged emotional immaturity and narcissism in the consultant will lead to an incapacity to adequately delineate self and object, internal and external realities. (as cited in Diamond, 2003, p. 9)

Although Levinson wrote extensively about many aspects of organizational assessment and change, most of his diagnostic and consultative approaches were oriented around a theoretical metaphor: use of psychodynamic clinical assessment methodologies essentially projected to the group and organizational levels and to the behavior of managers in organizations. Despite the many contributions Levinson's approaches have made to organizational diagnosis (see Diamond, 2003; Levinson, 2002a, 2002b, 2002c; Lowman, 2005), his was a translational (or metaphorical) approach, using models developed for individual-level work projected to the organizational level; therefore, it inevitably has limitations.

Ultimately, Levinson's model, like any other, has its uses and its limitations. He gets many points for having been one of the first psychologists to offer a theory-based approach to organizational-level consultation steeped in the pragmatic experiences of a highly experienced organizational consultant. And although Levinson could be persistent in his endorsement of the psychoanalytic concepts, they did not get in the way of his work with clients. His goals always were to help the client become more effective, to help remove barriers, and to further understanding.

Process Models

Chris Argyris's approach to consultation was briefly summarized in the last chapter. His approach to intervention theory (Argyris, 1971) was a process approach to organizational change. Argyris is also well known for his single- and double-loop learning models, which are largely prescriptive models for how organizations can learn to learn.

Another widely used process model is that of Edgar Schein (1998). This classic approach to consultation suggested that the goal of organizational consultation was not for the consultant to be an expert in the medical model but rather to facilitate the expertise held within the clients. This approach, like Argyris's (1971) model, is more oriented to helping others to help themselves and has been elaborated in Schein's important work of giving and receiving help and what he called "humble inquiry" (Schein, 2009, 2013).

Alderfer's Embedded Group Model

Another, more recent, theory-driven diagnostic model is that of Clayton Alderfer (2011), who published *The Practice of Organizational Diagnosis: Theory and Methods*, consolidating many of his approaches to organizational assessment. Although the book's title might suggest a generic approach to organizational diagnosis, by Alderfer's (2011) own description, however, the book follows "a theory that frames the dynamics of embedded intergroup relations . . . [examining] in detail the intricate interdependence between theory and method for understanding organizations" (p. xiii). In other words, Alderfer's is an organizational approach to assessment that focuses especially on the intersection of individuals, groups, and the organization as a whole using embedded intergroup relations theory as the model.

Alderfer's (2011) theory of embedded groups is an advanced theory with specific terms, models, propositions, hypotheses, and even "laws." Here's an example:

> Law 2: Interpersonal Relations as Intergroup Transactions. In any transaction with others, each individual—whether intending to or not—represents multiple identity (i.e., gender, race, family, sexual orientation, ethnicity, etc.) and organization (i.e., program, work-group, hierarchy, profession, etc.) groups. Which groups the person represents depends upon which people representing which other specific groups are present and on the relationship among those groups. (p. 242)

Using this approach, Alderfer helps organizational diagnosticians understand some of the complexity of the human parts of organizations. If individuals in groups really represent different identity groups (e.g., gender, age, race), then it follows that within work groups multiple groups are represented but also that those identity groups cut across an organization, in effect creating additional groups. Alderfer also helps consultants identify that what they see on the surface of individuals is less complex than what they may imagine. His approach aids consultants in understanding some of that complexity.

Ultimately, however, this model is about one or perhaps two major parts of organizations: groups and the relationship among them and individuals. It is not a comprehensive theory of organizational diagnosis, although it is a very useful one for thinking about those parts. The model illustrates the complexity of conducting assessments that will be representative of the organization and provides some practical suggestions for organizational entry using Alderfer's (2011) model.

Survey Methodology

Regardless of the particular theory involved in organizational/systemic change, survey data will often be used to objectively capture the attitudes and opinions of groups of employees and of the organization as a whole.

This is the forte of organizational and consulting psychologists, since they usually focus on the people of the organization.

This assessment approach was initially developed by the Bureau of Applied Social Research, the National Opinion Research Center, and the Survey Research Center of the ISR (Converse, 1987/2009). Commercial uses of survey research methodology were developed by George Gallup (e.g., 1976) and Donald Clifton (1999). Clifton's company eventually merged with the Gallup corporation after George Gallup's death (Lowman, 2004). Although the company is known most widely for its opinion polling in presidential and other political elections in the United States, that is a small part of the business, most of which focuses on surveys associated with for-profit companies. A famous 12-item measure of employee engagement, the Gallup Q^{12}, is typical of this work (see Harter, Schmidt, & Keyes, 2003; Harter, Schmidt, Killham, & Agrawal, 2009). Well-designed and validated surveys (see Fields, 2013) provide the opportunity to rapidly understand the attitudes and opinions of the organization as a whole, as well as its constituent parts, and the potential to track changes over time. When consulting with large organizations on attitudinal issues, the use of some types of survey methodology in assessing an organization may have few substitutes. Surveys and survey-guided feedback provide efficient ways to understand employee attitudes throughout even huge and complex organizations.

Case 10: Assessing an Entire Organization

A large government agency began a systemwide effort to assess employee attitudes on an annual basis. This was part of an effort to include the satisfaction and motivation of work groups, among other variables, as targeted goals for management. An internal consulting psychologist was assigned oversight of the project. She assembled a team of representatives from all levels in the agency to provide guidance on the project and to help determine the parameters for the project. The psychologist identified several possible instruments that could be used, and ultimately one that was developed for use in government settings was chosen. Each organizational unit in the agency that participated in the assessment project could work with the psychologist to add up to five items to the survey.

Because of the sensitivity of the data being collected, the consulting psychologist and the team of representatives decided (and the head of the agency agreed) that all data would be maintained under the control of the psychologist's office. Data would be analyzed at the agencywide, organizational unit, and group levels and would be receive feedback only in face-to-face meetings with a trained facilitator. When problems were identified, a specialist in organizational consultation would be made available. The survey would be administered annually for at least the next 5 years.

Results of the first annual survey identified several organizational units whose results were of concern. The psychologist met with the unit heads and helped them understand the results and what could be done about them. Two of the heads were not interested in organizational consultation and felt that the results reflected the chronic tendency of government employees to be "whiners and complainers." The agency head, who had access to the overall results, broken down by overall organizational units, was unhappy with the results and initiated an organizational development program. He put improvement in employee attitudes in the annual goals of each of the unit heads whose results were less than desirable.

This case illustrates a lot of the complexity involved in creating and administering a robust survey feedback program. The psychologist was careful and thoughtful in her approach, knowing some of the pitfalls that can occur in such work. The fact that the surveys were efficient in identifying problematic areas within the agency proved the utility of the assessment but alone did not solve the identified concerns. Assessment data help to identify problems but they do not solve them. The long-term approach taken by the agency was wise and puts less pressure on any one assessment. Still, such systems should not be used without commitment to address the issues identified by the findings.

Cultural Assessment

Another set of issues on which organizations can be assessed is the organization's culture, that is, the commonly held values, beliefs, and principles of those in the organization. The contributions of Denison (e.g., Denison, Hooijberg, Lane, & Lief, 2011), Schein (2010), and Cameron and Quinn

(2011) are helpful in showing the parameters of organizational culture, its assessment, and ways to intervene.

INTERVENTIONS

The literature has no shortage of organizational-level intervention approaches. (See, e.g., Cummings & Worley, 2014, for an up-to-date review of the organization development [OD] literature.) Many of these approaches focus on a particular subsystem of the organization, and most address issues related to parts of, not the whole, organization or to particular methodologies.

Process Versus Structural Approaches

Process approaches, as the term is used by psychologists, refers to interventions that are less focused on content and more on the ways in which people interact with each other and make decisions. Such an approach considers the client to have the answers if he or she can only discover a way to access that knowledge and to work around barriers that may impede awareness or understanding.

Structural approaches usually deal with making changes in the subparts of an organization, such as in the technology, the defined groups and reporting relationships in the organization, the degree to which power is widely dispersed within the organization, the design of jobs, and the person–machine interface. Employee involvement committees that are laid over existing structures would also be examples of such interventions.

These topics may or may not be within the consulting psychologist's areas of competence. Often, in major change efforts, psychologists in larger organizational projects will work on interdisciplinary teams to execute the interventions.

Consulting to Different Types of Organizations

Consulting psychologists who have experience working in multiple types of organizations will better understand how to apply their techniques and methods to a variety of specific situations and in different contexts. The methods and techniques for assessment and intervention apply, in principle, to all organizations, but once a consulting psychologist has seen the same conceptual phenomenon in multiple types of organizations, diagnosis can be faster and done with greater self-assurance.

Each type of organization (e.g., manufacturing, social service, hospitals, not-for-profit) has its own cultures, preferred or prescribed structures, and expectations of employees. Hospitals (Levin, 2002), for example, are highly regulated organizations with clear boundaries by professional groups (e.g., physicians, nurses, psychologists) as to allowable activities, span of control, allowed authority, and decision making, which will likely change some of the culture over time (in the United States, the Patient Protection and Affordable Care Act [2010] aims to focus more on team development and hospital-wide outcomes [Brown et al., 2015; Mechanic, 2012; Taplin, Foster, & Shortell, 2013]). Consulting psychologists working with for-profit organizations must often learn about a culture quite distinct from the health care or educational institutions in which they developed their skills and training as psychologists. Brock (2002) noted how the goals and mission of for-profit organizations affect power distribution, language, and culture and serve to create a "strategic triangle" of the company, its competitors, and its customers. Grabow (2002) discussed how consultants to for-profit organizations need to be managed by the company in a chapter that is instructive to consulting psychologists. Schools are typically hybrid organizations serving multiple missions, but a literature has developed on consulting to them (Dowd-Eagle & Eagle, 2014; Rosenfield & Humphrey, 2012). National security agencies (Civiello, 2009) present still another culture, including norms of secrecy, hiding of information from those outside the organization, and having to work with both politicians and military personnel.

Still other types of organizations needing specialized knowledge for consulting are family businesses (see Kaslow, 2006). Often, the dynamics of how work gets done in such settings is complicated by the dynamics of the family relationships. It is not surprising that in such companies, family members are often privileged compared with other employees when it comes to hiring and promotional practices. Conflict may be suppressed because nonfamily employees, fearing retaliation, may be reluctant to say what they really think about family members. Particularly alarming from the perspective of organizational survival is the finding that fewer than half of family businesses are successfully passed on to the next generation of family members, and of those, fewer than 15% are passed on to the third generation (Eddy, 1996).

Case 11: One Big, Not So Happy, Family

A consulting psychologist was asked to consult with the senior management team of a medium-sized organization that was experiencing a decline in its productivity. The company was led by a member of the family that owned the organization. One of these family members was the current president and two others were on the 12-person senior management team. One was responsible for finance; the other, for the purchasing department. The president highly competent and had earned his way up the organizational ladder. The other two siblings were widely regarded as placeholders, in their positions solely because of their family connections and after having had unsuccessful careers in other organizations doing work unrelated to their present jobs. The consulting psychologist suggested that individual interviews be conducted with all members of the executive team before proceeding with work with the team. Those interviews uncovered considerable blame attribution and unhappiness with the team, and the nonfamily employees felt they were being held back by the poor performance of the "incompetent" family members. The psychologist summarized the findings to the team and led them through a series of meetings in which the focus was on identifying the source of the current problems and developing a strategy for moving forward to solve them. The team was guided through a strategic planning process to help identify what steps were needed to compete more effectively in the marketplace. Some of the data that were developed for the work by the two family members was problematic (error-ridden, poorly done), and in time it became apparent to the president that they were part of the problem. He eased them out of their respective roles and found another place for them where their work would be less problematic. The consulting psychologist worked with the team to process the reactions to those changes and to help onboard the replacements. As the turnaround accelerated, the consulting psychologist was asked to expand the consulting work to other parts of the organization.

Other Organizational-Level Interventions

A variety of types of situations may also call for consulting psychologists to facilitate effective change. Mergers and acquisitions (e.g., De Meuse, Marks, & Dai, 2011; Marks & Mirvis, 2012) call for psychologists' expertise in assessing persons in the merged firm in helping managers decide who will be kept on after the merger. Merging the cultures of two or more organizations is difficult work, and often the mergers are not successfully executed (see King, Dalton, Daily, & Covin, 2004). Diversity interventions designed to address problems experienced by underrepresented groups and problems associated with globalization are discussed in Chapter 6 of this volume.

Outcomes of Organizational-Level Interventions

The effectiveness of organizational-level interventions has been examined mostly on an individual firm or consultant basis (see Winum, Nielsen, & Bradford, 2002) or in academic studies of what works and does not work at the organizational level. Halfhill, Huff, Johnson, Ballentine, and Beyerlein (2002) provided a useful overview of interventions that were more and less effective in their chapter "Interventions That Work (and Some That Don't): An Executive Summary of the Organizational Change Literature." A more recent review of the effectiveness of the OD literature is found in Woodman, Bingham, and Yuan (2008).

SUMMARY

Consulting at the organizational level adds to the complexity of working at the individual and group levels. When consulting with organizations, psychologists should determine the particular systems and subsystems in the organization that are to be the specific focus of their particular inter-ventions. The complexity of this level of work often requires working in teams, including with those from other professions.

Assessments often derive from theories of organizations and of peo-ple, but in large and complex organizations, survey methodologies may simply be used to efficiently assess employee points of view. Interventions should depend on the particular problems addressed. Some interventions have been carefully evaluated as to their general effectiveness but every intervention should have some form of outcome assessment.

5

Integrating Across Domains and Levels: The Case of Leadership

Using the individual–group–organizational level model of consulting psychology, many different variables need to be considered when working with organizations. Consulting psychologists can certainly choose to specialize in a particular level and, within that level, in the assessment or the intervention side (see Chapter 4, this volume). However, they must still know enough about the other levels to understand how issues at those levels may be affecting other aspects of the intervention. Additionally, issues are often interactive and not confined to one level.

In this chapter, I address consulting work that crosses levels and, within a level, that crosses variables. The chapter begins with the complex issue of leadership, one of the important issues of organizational consultation. Leadership, too, can be treated as a characteristic of individuals, a group phenomenon, or an organizational-level dimension. People who oversee others or who work in leadership roles can emphasize the day-to-day

http://dx.doi.org/10.1037/14853-005
An Introduction to Consulting Psychology: Working With Individuals, Groups, and Organizations,
by R. L. Lowman

goal orientation of getting the job done efficiently and effectively or take the organization in new directions. I differentiate in this chapter between managing and leading and between managing/leading and entrepreneurship. First, however, I focus on the general concept of leadership—influencing others to get work done in the context of organizations.

LEADERSHIP AND MANAGING OTHERS

Organizations require leadership for their sustained existence (see Kaiser, Hogan, & Craig, 2008). Historians (e.g., Burns, 1956, 1960; Caro, 2013) have meticulously considered every nuance of the personalities, abilities, values, and environmental influences of world leaders. Many theories of leadership have been promulgated, including those based on personality characteristics (e.g., Judge, Bono, Ilies, & Gerhardt, 2002; Judge, Piccolo, & Kosalka, 2009), on having relevant interests (Holland, 1997), and on being well matched to particular situations (contingency models; e.g., Fiedler, 2002; Fiedler & Chemers, 1987).

As a group, psychologists may not themselves be naturally inclined to be leaders. Indeed, much of the training of psychologists focuses on mastery of individual-level activities—mastery of knowledge and learning techniques and methods for which they are individually responsible. Considering the distribution of psychologists and the rather high number whose careers focus on providing individual or group mental health services, issues of leadership and the roles of leaders may not be a central interest. This is a concern when psychologists move into consultative roles because leadership is one of the central functions of organizations. Understanding leadership and power dynamics is particularly important.

Leadership also provides a good example of the importance of conceptualizing issues across organizational levels. It is not just psychologists who often think of leadership as a characteristic of individuals. Often organizations similarly conceptualize leaders at the individual level. Does this person have what it takes to be a good leader? Is this person going to be able to take the group (or organization) forward in the desired directions? What are the strengths and weaknesses of this person? At best, they ask: How good is the fit of this leader to this organization/group and to this particular role? But rarely do employers ask: Do we (or does this group) have what it takes to be well led? What do we need to do to make this leader's tenure be successful? or How do the person's strengths and weaknesses relate to those of the group/organization?

Considerable research has been conducted on psychological traits and other characteristics of managers and leaders judged to have been good or not good in such roles. Assuredly, some individuals even in the most favorable of circumstances would still most likely be ineffective leaders. They may not be smart enough for complex leadership roles (Schmidt & Hunter, 2004), they may have a personality disorder or the "wrong" personality for the role (R. Hogan, 2006), be low on empathy (Goleman, 1998), or simply have no managerially relevant interests (Sternberg, 1997)—and those characteristics are unlikely to change. But beyond the obvious misfits for leadership roles of any kind, individuals with reasonably strong "leadership profiles" can still be well suited for leadership positions in some groups or organizations and poorly suited for others.

In my own case, for example, I trained to be a psychologist, but before that I had an undergraduate degree in business and experience in management. I served as an administrator in the U.S. Air Force, and upon leaving the military, pursued a second bachelor's degree in psychology before attending graduate school. Since becoming a psychologist, I have pursued a career both in and out of academia, and in the latter positions I usually end up in some kind of leadership role. My interests are well focused when it comes to leadership: I like and do best with start-ups (of programs, groups, organizations) and turnarounds (taking things more near extinction to survival in relatively short time periods). I quickly become bored with static jobs or those in which success is determined by political skills. So, for some leadership roles I am well suited, and for others I am poorly matched. Yet, in terms of relatively stable interest–ability–personality characteristics, I have pretty much been the same person in both well- and less-good-fitting jobs.

LEADERSHIP AS A CHARACTERISTIC OF INDIVIDUALS

Much of personnel psychology as applied to the selection for leaders centers on assessing individual job candidates for possible hire or promotion on the basis of individual-level work analyses or job descriptions. These are roles consulting psychologists often take on. Individuals are assessed using robust ability–personality (or, increasingly, interest–ability–personality) variables that predict across a broad range of settings. Using outcome criteria, such as measurement of job performance on rating scales, these assessments (particularly of ability and intelligence; see Ones, Dilchert, Viswesvaran, & Salgado, 2010; Schmitt, 2014) have an impressive track record. Yet, emerging evidence suggests that in certain positions, particularly for high-level jobs, goodness of fit to the idiosyncratic needs of the organization at a particular point in time may be valuable (see, e.g., James & McIntyre, 2010).

When conceptualizing leadership at the individual level, the focus is on measurable characteristics of individuals that have shown predictive power in successful performance in the role of manager or executive. We use the interdomain model to frame the question (Lowman, 1991, 1993b; see also Carson, 1998; Randahl, 1991; Schmidt, 2014) and are therefore concerned about occupational interests, abilities, and personality. The question of predictability is a complicated one because variables in each of these domains have demonstrated predictive power on their own, but the exact manner of combining these variables across domains to maximize the predictive power is not well established. Nevertheless, evidence of incremental validity of combining across abilities, personality, and increasingly of interests (Van Iddekinge, Putka, & Campbell, 2011) indicates that measuring in multiple domains results in a better correlation with the outcome criteria than when measuring just within the area of the single best predictor.

The three classes of psychological variables with the best predictive power for managerial job performance are abilities, personality, and interest–fit and within each of these the following specific variables have shown a relationship with managerial performance.

Abilities

General Intelligence

General intelligence (Hunt, 2011; Schmidt, 2002; Schmidt & Hunter, 2004) remains the single best predictor of job performance in most fields, and leaders do not appear to be an exception. General intelligence rises with each level reached in the organization, so intelligence also predicts, among managers, how far one is likely to rise in hierarchical organizations. It provides the ability to learn quickly, to understand what needs to be done, and to understand the context in which leadership decisions are embedded. Additionally, ability variables described below have good evidence of their predictive power for managers.

Emotional Intelligence

Emotional intelligence (EI; Goleman, 1998; Mayer, Salovey, & Caruso, 2008) is widely used in assessing managerial candidates. Not without controversy as to what it is really measuring and its distinctiveness from general intelligence, EI is said to define managers' abilities to read the reactions of others, to respond in an emotionally and socially appropriate way to others, and (among other characteristics) to behave with others in an appropriate manner.

Prioritizing and Organizing

Called *administrative abilities* in the Howard and Bray (1988) longitudinal study of AT&T managers, prioritizing and organizing under time constraints is an important part of managers' jobs. Such skills are often measured in managerial simulations, including by the widely used in-basket simulation (Meyer, 1970).

Spatial Ability

The ability to visualize shapes and objects and to mentally rotate them or view them from different perspectives is important for many technical/ scientific jobs and technical managerial positions (Wai, Lubinski, & Benbow, 2009).

Personality

Conscientiousness

Conscientiousness (Barrick, Mount, & Judge, 2001) and its facet scales of need for achievement (or need for advancement; Hough & Dilchert, 2010; Hough, Ones, & Viswesvaran, 1998; Howard & Bray, 1988) and dependability/dutifulness (Oswald & Hough, 2011) is a personality variable that has the best track record in predicting to job performance. Disaggregating this broad summary variable into its component parts (so-called facet scales or dimensions of the larger trait), it appears that dependability best predicts to job performance and need for achievement predicts to advancement (Ones, Dilchert, Viswesvaran, & Judge, 2007). This assumes that dependability is a facet scale of conscientiousness, which not all researchers (see Hough & Dilchert, 2010; Roberts, Chernyshenko, Starks, & Goldberg, 2005) agree upon.

Extraversion/Introversion

Extraversion (Judge et al., 2002) and its presumed facets of agency (potency; Minbashian, Bright, & Bird, 2009) and assertiveness (Hough et al., 1998; Oswald & Hough, 2011), along with introversion, is a broad-brush (Big Five) personality dimension that encompasses a number of facet scales. Managers generally work with lower to midlevel supervisors and with other managers. Extreme introversion may interfere with the ability to work effectively with such contexts. On the other hand, it may create less difficulty if the work involves overseeing other introverts (as technical people often are) versus highly extraverted people. Facet scales may do a better job of predicting to specific job duties and raise fewer applicant concerns than measuring only the overall (and presumably relatively unchangeable) higher level extraversion/introversion variable.

Integrity and Absence of Personality Disorder or Neuroticism

Integrity (see Barrick, Mount, & Judge, 2001; Berry, Sackett, & Wiemann, 2007; R. Hogan, 2006; Lowman, 1989; Van Iddekinge, Roth, Raymark, & Odle-Dusseau, 2012) tests predict especially well to counterproductive work behavior. This includes stealing, lying, and challenging authority. Neuroticism is a Big Five personality variable that encompasses anxiety and depression (supposedly within the normal range of personality).

Except for some aspects of creative work, it generally predicts less effective workplace performance. The trait can conversely be labeled as emotional stability, in which case it is positively associated with job performance.

Occupational (Vocational) Interests

Prototypical Managerial Interest Profile: Enterprising–Social–Conventional

Match of interests with position (Nye, Su, Rounds, & Drasgow, 2012; Van Iddekinge et al., 2011) is an important aspect of organizational success (see Holland, 1997).

Occupational interests (see Lowman & Carson, 2003, 2012) identify patterns of liking of various activities, including occupations. They are quite stable over time and are increasingly being examined as a variable adding incremental variance predicting both job performance and satisfaction, especially when measured in terms of fit with the organization. In the case of managers, the most highly elevated interests on average are enterprising–conventional–social (O*NET, n.d.-a). This interest profile suggests comfort with overseeing and directing others, liking of business and managerial activities, willingness to do things in a standardized way, and a liking of social and interpersonal activities. Conversely, this profile suggests less attraction to things scientific, creative, or hands on.

Variations in Interest Profiles

Although the prototypical interest profile for nontechnical managers emphasizes Enterprising–Social–Conventional interest themes, there are exceptions. In technical companies in which a degree or advanced training in a technical specialty is required, managers may be likely to have technical (e.g., Realistic–Investigative–Enterprising) rather than generic managerial interest profiles. The work to be managed in such settings may mean that there is more technical ability needed to be an effective supervisor. Another variation can be exhibited in secondary or tertiary codes. For example, while generic managers may exhibit Enterprising–Social–Conventional, profiles in sales or marketing may bring in Artistic codes, such as, Enterprising–Social–Artistic. This reflects the need for flexibility and comfort with unstructured approaches to creating, for example, a connection with prospective clients or in selling or marketing a product.

INTEGRATING ACROSS
INTEREST–ABILITY–PERSONALITY VARIABLES

Summarizing the relative importance of the variables just listed, extensive studies and research findings about predictors of managerial performance suggest that abilities are of most importance in predicting managerial and leadership success. Within abilities, general intelligence is persistently the strongest predictor. Personality variables are also important, but only selected ones of the five major factors, and in some cases, facet scales rather than the overarching Big Five personality variables. Occupational interests are the sleeper variable starting to show increasing relevance.

Note that these are relatively stable characteristics that accurately predict job performance outcomes at the individual level. But all of these are different in kind from the measurement of leadership competencies, the presumably trainable managerial and leadership day-to-day skills (even if they build on underlying abilities such as intelligence and conscientiousness).

If, as this list suggests, there are multiple predictors of managerial success, with differing levels of correlation with job performance criteria, the choice of predictors is not "either/or." Rather, multiple variables can be used to maximize the aggregated variance in the outcome measures explained by the predictors.

Still, with each added variable that potentially contributes incremental validity evidence, the question of how to combine across multiple dimensions is complex when making predictions about real people. A simple quantitative approach might be used with differential weighting of predictors when assessing groups of candidates for the same positions if the sample sizes are large enough to have validated the relative weighting of the various predictors.

In practice, without using a validity generalization approach, sample sizes for selecting managers and leaders, particularly high-level ones, are often small and the outcome criteria limited. And, as James and McIntyre

(2010) noted, managerial positions do not necessarily fit well into validity generalization models when the degree of fit of person to job and organization may be idiosyncratic.

In predicting to performance outcomes associated with alternative leadership approaches, the emphasis is on group-level or organization-wide performance. This helps to ensure statistical power and to have more robust findings about the association of predictors and criteria. Multiple predictors can be analyzed to determine the relative contributions to the criterion of the various predictors to maximize the association between predictors and criterion.

In practice, however, when psychological assessments or assessment centers are used, multiple measures of broad-spectrum abilities (e.g., cognitive abilities) and broad-spectrum personality measures (e.g., those based on the Big Five measures of personality) are administered. It is not atypical for such assessments to be conducted and interpreted by consultants or consulting firms, often using standard test instruments. The assessment process results in a report for the client organization summarizing the results of assessment, cautions about hiring, and possibly issues that should be taken into account should the candidate be hired. Possibly, the firm summarizes the data with a three-point scale: don't hire, proceed with caution, or hire. Employers may like such a reduction in complexity, and the system may lend itself to a somewhat automated process on the part of assessors. But the process may inadvertently use a nonvalidated way of combining across predictors or leave to the prospective employer the job of integrating information about a number of different variables that may result in the assessment either effectively not being used or the results made use of in an idiosyncratic way.

Let us now turn to the issue of rule-out versus rule-in predictors. R. Hogan, J. Hogan, Kaiser, and colleagues (e.g., J. Hogan, R. Hogan, & Kaiser, 2011; Kaiser, Hogan, & Craig, 2008; Kaiser, LeBreton, & Hogan, 2015), perhaps a bit exuberantly, estimated that managerial failure, including unethical behavior or, in effect, personality disorders, is massive (as high as 60%). (For another view, suggesting bright sides to some dark sides of personality characteristics, see Furnham, Trickey, & Hyde, 2012.) Rule-out criteria relate to identifying bad or potentially bad behaviors and personal variables that, no matter what the talents or personality and interest fit may otherwise be, would be a basis for not hiring or promoting a candidate. Persons with personality disorders may treat people inappropriately or may ultimately take high risks with the organization that result in later problems or even in the firm's catastrophic failure. Yet, such characteristics may be paired with excellent abilities and even normal or desirable characteristics of personality. Such leaders may be charismatic and well-regarded when their pathology does not kick in.

Another approach to using more than one predictor sequentially is called a multistage, or multiple hurdles, approach (see, e.g., Finch, Edwards, & Wallace, 2009). In this method, applicants must pass a series of steps before being in the final pool of people from among whom the accepted applicants will be chosen. Of course, most selection processes are multistage in approach. Usually, applicants apply for a job, and many are rejected for various reasons (e.g., lack of relevant qualifications, degrees, etc.) at that step. Next may then be an initial interview with a human resources (HR) professional who may screen in or out candidates. Perhaps references and verification processes will occur next and others eliminated. An initial, unproctored Internet-based testing might then occur. In-person proctored testing might occur next under the supervision of psychologists (Wunder, Thomas, & Luo, 2010). Those making it to this point in the process may then be interviewed by managers, and the candidate selected at this point. Provisional employment offers might be made, and then if job relevant, further screening (psychological or medical) might occur.

Clearly, it is cleaner and easier to use a single variable to predict to a single-outcome criterion. But we know that intelligence, if that were to be the one variable that would be used, is insufficient for purposes of predicting leadership performance and indeed for many kinds of work-related performance. Yet, the issues in combining across multiple measures to make selection decisions are complex (see J. W. Johnson & Oswald, 2010).

Managerial Versus Leadership Competencies

Management at its core is about getting things done, usually in a social or organizational context, working with and through other people. Leadership is about motivating, inspiring others, setting a direction and help-ing people see the value in the new directions. Managers may differ from leaders in some important ways, but it may make more sense to speak of management and leadership functions rather than of people, because to some extent, managers have to be leaders and leaders have to be manag-ers. I begin with a discussion of management functions.

Recognized as being the founder of management, Peter Drucker, a journalist, prolific and influential writer, academic, and consultant, said in his 1954 path breaking book *The Practice of Management*: "A manager *sets objectives*—A manager *organizes*—A manager *motivates and communicates*—A manager, by establishing yardsticks, *measures*—A man-ager *develops people*" (Drucker, 1954/1982, p. 344). Similarly, Boyatzis (1982) noted that "at the core of every manager's job is the requirement to make things happen toward a goal or consistent with a plan. Managers need to set goals and initiate actions to achieve them" (p. 60). But achiev-ing goals is not done on one's own. It involves bringing together resources and people to help achieve the goals. It involves being able to prioritize—to decide what needs to be done first, second, and next. And it involves an incessant need to see that things get done on a deadline.

This introduces the concept of management and leadership from the perspective not of personal and psychological characteristics of people that predict well to managerial job performance but rather from the job duties that managers actually do on a day-to-day basis. Along with this is the question of the presumably learnable skills that need to be mastered to be effective in the job.

One of the best resources in the world for identifying characteristics of jobs and the skills needed by people to do jobs is the U.S. Department of Labor's O*NET (n.d.-b), a systematic, empirically derived, compendium of a vast array of jobs and occupations. For the job categories of General and Operations Managers (11-1021.00 in the O*NET system; O*NET, n.d.-a) the brief job description is

> Plan, direct, or coordinate the operations of public or private sector organizations. Duties and responsibilities include formulating poli-cies, managing daily operations, and planning the use of materials

and human resources, but are too diverse and general in nature to be classified in any one functional area of management or administration, such as personnel, purchasing, or administrative services. (para. 1)

Specific O*Net identified job duties are also identified. Examples include:

oversee activities directly related to making products or providing services and

direct and coordinate activities of businesses or departments concerned with the production, pricing, sales, or distribution of products. (Tasks, items 2–3)

The following skills (competencies) needed to be able to do these job duties are identified by the O*Net:

- active listening,
- reading comprehension,
- speaking,
- critical thinking,
- monitoring,
- coordination,
- social perceptiveness,
- active learning,
- complex problem solving, and
- judgment and decision making.

Leaders Versus Managers

To this point, I have used the words *leaders* and *managers* more or less interchangeably. As noted at the start of this section, however, all managers are not leaders and all leaders are not necessarily good managers. The distinction between managerial and leadership skills was first influentially identified by Peter Drucker in the widely quoted phrase "Management is doing things right: leadership is doing the right things" (as cited in Covey, 1989, p. 101). Knowing what to do to lead an organization or group forward is what leadership emphasizes; getting things done working with and through others to accomplish goals is what management is. This implies perhaps that managers can to some degree be trained to be more leader like and leaders more attentive to managerial duties. Ironically, as people rise in a managerial hierarchy, the job is less about management and more about leadership. Paradoxically, the skill set that caused managers to have success in moving up the ladder may not be what is needed at the higher levels of the organization.

Entrepreneurs Versus Managers

Another distinction that should be explicitly made is about entrepreneurship versus management. Entrepreneurs are those who start new businesses or programs and who excel at creating things that did not previously exist. They create new products, programs, and businesses and are generally resilient to what others would see as failures. Again, most managers are not entrepreneurs and most entrepreneurs are not the best managers, but the differences do not reside in persons in a way that is impervious to change.

That said, entrepreneurs often have a characteristic personality type that differentiates them from managers, but of course not all entrepreneurs are alike. Although it is difficult on the basis of current research findings to find entirely predictable common characteristics among entrepreneurs (see Low & MacMillan, 1988; Stuetzer, Obschonka, & Schmitt-Rodermund, 2013), some of the more promising commonalities or trends include:

1. role identity and early experiences as an entrepreneur (Krueger, 2007);
2. escalation of commitment (willingness to work very hard and usually longer hours than those in salaried positions; Baron, 2000; Jamal, 1997);
3. high needs for autonomy and preference for doing what one wants to do (Benz & Frey, 2008; Feldman & Bolino, 2000);
4. strong (sometimes overly strong) confidence (Baron, 2000; Busenitz & Barney, 1997; Yang & Danes, 2015);
5. strong (sometimes overly strong) optimism (Ucbasaran, Westhead, & Wright, 2011);
6. high tolerance of ambiguity (Low & MacMillan, 1988);

7. social competence (among more successful entrepreneurs; Baron, 2000); and

8. tendency to be overly optimistic, including to view "failures" as a necessary part of entrepreneurship (Lowe & Ziedonis, 2006).

A good deal of speculation and stereotypes have surrounded entrepreneurs. Zaleznik and de Vries (1976), using a psychoanalytic framework, described the entrepreneur this way:

> The entrepreneur is a kind of psychological gambler. At the times of their greatest setbacks, many of these entrepreneurs seem to feel their best. Their unconscious belief is that, since they have finally been punished for their success, the worst is over. The resulting sense of relief from anxiety and guilt stirs them into fresh activities, starting anew the process of constructing an enterprise. (p. 22)

Entrepreneurs have also been characterized by empirical researchers as having elements of narcissistic personality (Mathieu & St-Jean, 2013). Mathieu and St-Jean (2013) noted that some elements of narcissism are positive and others not. For example, part of narcissism can reflect high self-confidence or the willingness to pursue one's own objectives. In an interesting study of CEOs' narcissism and company performance, Wales, Patel, and Lumpkin (2013) found that entrepreneurial orientation served as a mediator of the relationship with narcissism and firm performance, helping to explain the variable relationship found in prior studies between narcissism and firm performance.

Such views and findings reflect a tendency among some professionals and the lay public alike to attribute complex, often idiosyncratic, motivations to entrepreneurs. It is important, however, not to generalize from extremely successful entrepreneurs to the class as a whole and to focus only on perceived problematic motivations or behaviors. What does seem to hold true is that entrepreneurs as a group are willing to take risks that may not seem like risks to them and to have higher tolerance than others for what may be perceived as failure. Although such motivations may differentiate them from the population at large they may be necessary to create new things and are not necessarily malevolently motivated.

Other, more positive predictors of the performance of entrepreneurs, have also been found. Yang and Danes (2015) found that entrepreneurs' new business development success was predicted by business confidence and positive life outlook but also by an economic variable (business demand), which had a curvilinear relationship with the criterion.

Clearly all entrepreneurs are not created equally (Carree & Verheul, 2012). There are individual differences among entrepreneurs and some who might be labeled as entrepreneurs because they run their own businesses but may not have done so as their first choice. Block, Sandner, and Spiegel (2015) differentiated these types of entrepreneurs as opportunity entrepreneurs and necessity entrepreneurs. The latter are those who are forced by circumstances to become entrepreneurs, whereas the former intentionally seek it out.

The major points to be made here are that managers and leaders are not necessarily entrepreneurs and that generalizations about managers and possibly leaders may require separate approaches because their profiles may differ.

LEADERSHIP AS A GROUP-LEVEL PHENOMENON

In taking leadership as an example to illustrate the complexity of real-life applications, I have to this point primarily discussed interdomain and between-variables relationships at a single level—the individual level. Reviewing these relationships is complicated enough, but I also want to emphasize that leadership is a variable that is manifest at the group and organizational levels as well.

At the group level, leadership is viewed not primarily as a role within a group that derives from individual-level characteristics (although those can be relevant). Rather, leadership is viewed as a property of behavior in groups that may attach to a single person or to multiple individuals.

Leadership has been studied as a small-group phenomenon, particularly by social psychologists. Shaw (1971) stated the following:

> The leadership role is one of the most important roles associated with positions in the group structure. It has been studied more extensively than any other role and with the greatest variety of research

techniques. It is probably also true that 'leader' and 'leadership' have been defined in more different ways than almost any other concept associated with group structure. (p. 267)

After reviewing a number of definitions of *group leader* he proposed his own: "the leader [is] that group member who exerts positive influence over other group members, or as that member who exerts more positive influence than they exert over him" (Shaw, 1971, p. 269)

In work group applications, groups typically have assigned leaders who are usually selected by management. Such individuals may have been carefully chosen to identify those who are skilled with working with people and who have the necessary temperament to function effectively at the interface between employees and management. Or they may be selected on the basis of people competing for the job because that is the only way for them to get pay raises or to rise up the hierarchy. Or they may be someone favored by the person(s) making the selection decisions.

Hackman and Wageman (2005) argued that however the formal leaders are chosen, and whether there are informal leaders who help get the group's work done, work group effectiveness could be judged against the following three criteria:

1. The productive output of the team (i.e., its product, service, or decision) meets or exceeds the standards of quantity, quality, timeliness of the team's clients—the people who receive, review, and/or use the output. It is the clients' standards and assessments that count in assessing team products—not those of the team itself (except in rare cases where the team is the client of its own work) or those of the team's manager (who only rarely is the person who actually receives and uses a team's output).

2. The social processes the team uses in carrying out the work enhance members' capability of working together interdependently in the future. Effective teams become adept at detecting and correcting errors before serious damage is done and at noticing and exploiting emerging opportunities.

3. The group experience contributes positively to the learning and personal well-being of individual team members. Work teams can serve as sites for personal learning and can spawn satisfying interpersonal

relationships, but they also can deskill, frustrate, and alienate their members. We do not count as effective any team for which the net impact of the group experience on members' learning and well-being is more negative than positive. (p. 272; see also Hackman, 1987)

Hackman and Wageman went on to identify three ways in which groups or teams can influence team effectiveness:

1. the level of *effort* group members collectively expend carrying out task work,
2. the appropriateness to the task of the *performance strategies* the group uses in its work, and
3. the amount of *knowledge and skill* members bring to bear on the task. (p. 273)

At this level of analysis, we move beyond individual constructs and characteristics of leadership. Leadership is no longer defined as something inherent in or characteristic of a single, predefined leader but rather as a more dynamic process that changes over time and that must take into account the perceptions of the group as well as consideration of those with formal position power.

LEADERSHIP AT THE ORGANIZATIONAL LEVEL

Leadership can also be studied as an organizational (or even societal) level variable. If aspects of leadership at the group level are complex, at the organizational level of analysis, they are even more so.

Huge sums of money are spent on the salaries, benefits, and bonuses of CEOs of large corporations, but the connection between those expenditures and the direct results of the CEO's efforts are not always clear (see, e.g., Kolev, 2008). In an interesting study by Tosi, Misangyi, Fanelli, Waldman, and Yammarino (2004), the charisma of the CEO as rated by senior leadership in the CEO's corporations was compared with perceived charisma of the CEO in relationship to CEO compensation and firm performance. They found a direct relationship between rated charisma and CEO pay and no relationship with the firm's performance.

Other findings also dispute whether salaries paid to CEOs are reflective of any impact of the CEO on firm level outcomes (see Walsh, 2008). Wade, Porac, and Pollock (1997) found that compensation committees of boards adjusted their explanations to justify paying high compensation increases to CEOs, often ignoring that the available outcome data did not support the salaries being paid and certainly the nearly universal belief that there should be less discrepancy between the very high pay of senior executives and earnings of the rest of the employees (see Kiatpongsan & Norton, 2014).

So, although the added value of the CEOs of companies may not match the very high compensation they are being paid and leaders may be overpaid, leadership nonetheless is a constant preoccupation of organizations. Who is hired for senior leadership roles, how they are compensated, how they are performing, and how favor can be curried with them are frequent concerns in organizations. And, of course, consulting psychologists are often involved in working with leaders with the organizational level in mind.

When a highly paid executive's performance is at risk, a consultant may be called in for coaching. Consulting psychologists may be tasked with assessing and developing leaders at many levels of an organization. This work may involve assessment of leadership strengths throughout the organization or of specific groups or types of managers. Psychologists working with leaders at the organizational level may also be a good position to understand where the stressors are particularly acute and what is driving them. When a senior leader is dysfunctional or destructive, this can have adverse consequences throughout the organization.

POWER AND LEADERSHIP

Inevitably, leaders—almost by definition—have power over other people. They control both means and outcomes of others. Sometimes this is a function of a natural liking for the exercise of power and control over others but typically leaders and managers are driven more by the desire for achievement. However, leaders do need to be familiar with the power inherent in their leadership roles and understand how to use it in the service of the institutional goals (McClelland & Burnham, 1976/2003).

Because by and large psychologists are not particularly adept at or comfortable with the exercise of power, they may underestimate its importance and necessity. What gravitates them to helping and to knowledge-based roles often does not jive well with those who are motivated by the desire to control others. Greene's (1998) popular book *The 48 Laws of Power* includes among its laws the following:

- Never outshine the master.
- Never put too much trust in friends; learn how to use enemies.
- Conceal your intentions.
- Keep others in suspended terror; cultivate an air of unpredictability. (pp. ix–xi)

These are hardly rules that would be consistent with psychologists' values. Nonetheless, for centuries, power has been of interest to people who have it and to those who do not. Consulting psychologists do need to be familiar with how power is exercised and by whom in their consulting projects—including how those in power got it and how they have held (or lost) it.

SUMMARY AND CONCLUSION

This chapter addressed complex relationships that cut across levels (individual, group, organizational) and relationships within a level but that cut across variables within domains. Because these relationships are complicated, there are few easy or formulaic approaches when it comes to assessments or interventions in consulting psychology. In working with the context and complexity of the variables, psychologists can build on, but will likely need to extend, their focal areas of consulting psychology competence.

6

Multicultural and International Issues in Consulting Psychology

This chapter introduces some of the ways in which consulting psychologists should take into account multicultural and international issues in their work. This is an ethical responsibility (see Chapter 7, this volume, for more on ethics) but also a pragmatic one for organizational consulting psychologists.

When it comes to consulting psychology, multicultural competencies are necessary, yet the traditional U.S.-centric constructs of multiculturalism are not always sufficient. Consulting psychology work has become international, not just as an esoteric undertaking by a few select psychologists but, rather, as an aspect of many consulting psychologists' day-to-day work with clients. This is particularly true as electronic media has expanded, along with the growth of international companies. With worldwide clientele, consulting psychologists incur the obligation to become

http://dx.doi.org/10.1037/14853-006

An Introduction to Consulting Psychology: Working With Individuals, Groups, and Organizations, by R. L. Lowman interculturally competent (i.e., able to work with people from different cultures across countries and international populations within countries), rather than being only multiculturally competent (i.e., being able to work with people from different cultures within the United States). This adds complexity to the required knowledge base beyond that needed by those working primarily in one country. I return to these ideas in the next section, "Internationalism as a Multicultural Dimension."

Multicultural issues fall into two broad categories. The first category involves working with marginalized and oppressed employees to learn how companies and those within them can function in fairer and more equitable ways. The second category concerns addressing diversity issues as a source for positive outcomes for work groups and organizations, that is, helping organizations make the most of the diversity within them to create better outcomes. Much of the existing literature on multiculturalism has focused more on the former than on the latter. Yet, it is the job of the consulting psychologist both to be sensitive to issues of mistreatment of members of marginalized groups having experienced discrimination but also to work with multicultural issues, broadly defined, as a source of organizational excellence and competitive advantage.

As with any other psychologists, consulting psychologists' values and ethics commit them to be cognizant of multicultural differences and how their approaches apply to minorities, older persons, those with disabilities, and the many categories for which discrimination has long existed. These issues cannot be ignored in the context of organizations.

Although few would argue that those groups in the United States who have experienced discrimination, persecution, and denial of rights, including, in some cases, the very right to exist, do not uniformly have the status and protection they should, progress has been extensive—if more so for some groups than for others. Currently, concerns about protecting the rights and opportunities and equal treatment of individuals based on their physical disabilities (Olkin, 2002), sexual orientation (Kuba, 2013), immigration status (Arredondo & Rodriguez, 2006; Malos, 2012), national origin (Leach, Leong, Inman, & Ciftçi, 2013), and religion/nonreligion (Limberg, 2013) assume greater relevance and importance in schools, in society, and in work. Yet, despite the advances in multiculturalism, including establishing and enforcing the rights of all citizens, especially those who have been oppressed, much work remains to be done, and should be a concern of all psychologists (Eibach & Keegan, 2006).

Herndon (2013) addressed this gap with respect to one category of diversity, racism, by stating:

> Although racial progress is undeniable, 'it is not as broad or as deep as post-racialists would like to assert.' Contrary to post-racialism, it is unmistakable that racism still remains a major phenomenon in the United States today. Historic racial stratification can be seen in statistics that show that Blacks fare far worse than their white counterparts in terms of poverty, income, wealth, homeownership, employment, education, and criminal justice. Further, negative attitudes about Blacks continue to present themselves in multiple areas of life. (p. 334)

Consulting psychologists have many concerns about work inequities based on multicultural categories and differential treatment. For example, women workers chronically earn, on average, less than men (Coukos, 2012; Kalantari, 2012); African American men are overrepresented in prisons and underrepresented in the workplace, with higher levels of unemployment and lower salaries (U.S. Department of Labor, 2012); immigrants often are not able to work legally due to not having work permits or immigration status; and those who are both immigrants and minorities are underpaid compared with Whites (both White immigrants and White nonimmigrants; Stewart & Dixon, 2010).

But by and large, psychologists who work with organizations are not brought in to address such disparities. They are hired instead to consult with the organization or individuals on how to help the human side of the enterprise be more effective. Of course, some consulting psychologists will specialize in diversity and multiculturalism (see, e.g., Ferdman & Deane, 2014) and may provide coaching services to individuals from diverse backgrounds. But almost all consultants will need to be able to work successfully with individuals from a variety of cultural backgrounds. This is an ethical requirement as well as one deriving from a competency necessary to be effective in one's role as a consultant.

The American Psychological Association's (APA's; 2010) *Ethical Principles of Psychologists and Code of Conduct* (hereinafter, "Ethics Code") describes the ethics of competence:

> Where scientific or professional knowledge in the discipline of psychology establishes that an understanding of factors associated with age, gender, gender identity, race, ethnicity, culture, national origin, religion, sexual orientation, disability, language, or socioeconomic status is essential for effective implementation of their services or research, psychologists have or obtain the training, experience, consultation, or supervision necessary to ensure the competence of their services, or they make appropriate referrals, except as provided in Standard 2.02, Providing Services in Emergencies. (Standard 2.01b)

These, of course, are the multicultural categories that have been identified by U.S. psychologists, but the categories are generic enough to consider other not specifically recognized ones, such as immigration or employment status. Increasingly, however, consulting psychologists must seek—and develop—an understanding of how these issues and concerns apply to other cultures—not just those of the United States or Westernized nations. Whether working with clients through electronic media or in person, psychologists need a guide to help them understand the nature of, and to develop, relevant competencies to work with a wider and wider range of cultural issues.

INTERNATIONALISM
AS A MULTICULTURAL DIMENSION

Because today's companies are increasingly international (Lowman, 2013b), psychologists who work with them and their employees must be prepared to work with clients from a diversity of cultures and perspectives. This adds considerable complexity when psychologists work with employees all around the world.

As noted, much of the impetus for creating multiculturalism stemmed from the effort to correct wrongs and to require professionals to be multiculturally competent. Today, however, traditional categories of "righting wrongs" (the need for which has not gone away; see, e.g., Amodio & Devine, 2006; Binder et al., 2009; Devine, 1989) are being supplemented by cultural diversity competencies that are associated with the need to effectively manage a workforce that now knows no boundaries. Consulting psychologists who work with employees who do not neatly fit the current protected class categories (such as Iranian Americans or Guatemalan refugees who fled oppression in their native country or, in Turkey, the approximately 1.5 million Syrian refugees now residing there [United Nations High Commissioner for Refugees, 2015]) will need to expand their knowledge of diversity. National origin is a protected class in the United States but it has not received much attention as a group that does need class protection. Similarly, immigrants to the United States, particularly from Mexico, may raise special issues for consulting psychologists (see Arredondo & Rodriguez, 2006; see also, Dealberto, 2007).

On the other hand, no one can be expected to learn everything about all cultures and backgrounds in the world. As international companies and consulting firms are increasingly scattered around the world, opportunities may arise for working with many different cultures. What is important is not that the psychologist be fully informed about each cultural group but that he or she has a meta-understanding of how cultures in general differ as a basis on which to study, research, learn, and, if needed, to obtain relevant supervision for working with the new (to the consulting psychologist) culture. One of the earliest books in the current series Fundamentals of Consulting Psychology is Glover and Friedman's (2015) *Transcultural Competence: Navigating Cultural Differences in the Global Community*. Their pragmatic but theory-based model is organized around the "4 Rs" of Recognition (sensitivity to the differences around one), Respect (appreciating the differences), Reconciliation (ability to navigate around differences and, as appropriate, to resolve them), and Realization (the ability to implement actions based on resolution).

As these issues apply to international organizations, complex questions need to be considered. On the one hand, international companies have employees all over the world, many working in conditions of relative poverty compared with those in more economically advanced countries; consulting psychologists need to understand these companies in terms of their indigenous cultures. They must be careful not to make cultural assumptions or gaffes that would impede the consulting relationship.

On the other hand there is the issue to consider of whether international corporations are cultures of their own. It has been argued (e.g., Fulkerson, 2012; Lowman, 2012; White & Shullman, 2012) that when consulting psychologists work with individuals in corporations, corporate culture may in effect trump national culture. Employees of global corporations, although residing in many different countries, are often highly selected individuals with elite backgrounds who are seeking economic and social advancement and may therefore identify less with their own cultures than with the culture of the corporation itself and values related to advancement and achievement.

This does not, of course, mean that such individuals do not have multiple identities or conflicts at the intersections of these identities. Consulting psychologists and assessors need to be sensitive to internal conflicts that are often associated with identity changes such as those associated with economic advancement. These conflicts may be painful but not something that the employees necessarily feel safe or comfortable sharing or discussing. Additionally, when those being coached reside in less affluent countries than other corporate locations they may know (and resent) that they, as citizens of poorer countries, are earning less money than others for doing what they see as the same work (see Lopez & Ensari, 2013), resulting in possible unhappiness and internal conflict. These differences may be justified by the presumed lower costs of living, but for those at the managerial ranks, the costs of maintaining a Western-like standard of living may actually be higher than in the Western nations.

Power differentials may also be common, if implicit, among employees in the country in which the corporation is based versus in poorer countries in which branch offices may be located. These issues may be manifest in such seemingly minor details as the times meetings are scheduled (favoring the Western country locations and possibly forcing those in other locations persistently to be on calls from the workplace in the middle of their night; see Lopez & Ensari, 2013). Also, corporate officials may be oblivious to the perceived concerns of those in outlying countries working in management and professional positions about language issues (e.g., meetings conducted in English despite that not being the first language of many and without translators provided) or salary differentials and may assume employees' views to be different than they actually are, particularly in conflict-avoidant cultures.

MULTICULTURAL COMPETENCIES
FOR CONSULTING PSYCHOLOGY WORK

Various models have been put forward for multicultural competencies, including those related to internationalizing the field (see, e.g., Arredondo & Reinoso, 2003; Arredondo & Tovar-Blank, 2014; Lowman, 2013b). APA's relevant publications include the *Guidelines on Multicultural Education, Training, Research, Practice, and Organizational Change for Psychologists* (APA, 2003; hereinafter, "Multicultural Guidelines"). These Multicultural Guidelines provide nonenforceable guidance relevant for practicing psychologists. (The inclusion of "organizational change" in the title of these guidelines might suggest that they address the roles of psychologists whose work is as organizational development consultants; they do not.) Rather, the Multicultural Guidelines aim to address the necessity for psychologists to speak up about multicultural issues in their own organizations.

The Multicultural Guidelines note that psychologists are themselves "cultural beings" who may hold beliefs, including those outside of their conscious awareness, that affect their reactions to others, including clients. The Multicultural Guidelines specifically mention race and ethnicity but could apply equally well to most other multicultural categories, such as gender, sexual orientation, and religion or immigration status. They note the need for "culturally appropriate" skills in applied psychological work (Guideline 5; APA, 2003, p. 390). They also identify an obligation of psychologists to make use of organizational change processes in policy development (Guideline 6: Psychologists are encouraged to use organizational change processes to support culturally informed organizational [policy] development and practices; APA, 2003, p. 392). Again, these guidelines are not enforceable but may be cited in legal proceedings and certainly can be referenced with one's clients as a basis for particular action.

PUBLISHED ARTICLES, CHAPTERS, AND SPECIAL ISSUES

The Society of Consulting Psychology (APA Division 13) has published in its journal, *Consulting Psychology Journal: Practice and Research*, a number of articles and special issues on multicultural and particularly international issues in consulting. The special issues include:

- "International Organizational Consulting: Consulting Psychology Goes Global" (Cooper, 2012), which reviews with case examples the realities and challenges of performing consulting in international contexts and the lessons learned from those in the field doing this work;
- "Culture, Race, and Ethnicity in Organizational Consulting Psychology" (Cooper & Leong, 2008), which applies multicultural knowledge largely developed in other contexts to organizational consulting psychology; and
- "Implications of the ADA of 1990 for Psychologists" (O'Keeffe, 1993), which is a summary of the Americans With Disabilities Act and its implications for psychological practice.

MULTICULTURAL AND INTERNATIONAL COMPETENCIES OF LEADERS AND MANAGERS

The question arises as to whether multicultural and international competencies are specific skills needed by effective managers. Inceoglu and Bartram (2012), on the other hand, argued that it was not necessary to conceptualize a separate "multicultural competency" because the multicultural aspects of leaders working in international contexts can be conceptualized in terms of other required leadership competencies. They stated:

> Our view is that leadership competencies are leadership competencies across all situations; however, their scope needs to be broadened for a multicultural context. Such a context adds to the heterogeneity and complexity that leaders experience but is not different in kind to the other aspects of complexity with which leaders have to cope (e.g., dealing with different markets, different stakeholders, and different

levels of the organization). . . . Our conclusion is that the focus should be on specific competencies relevant for leadership effectiveness that can be expanded in terms of the range of behaviors they relate to for leadership in a global or multicultural context rather than viewing multicultural effectiveness as a separate, ill-defined competency. (pp. 216–218)

SUMMARY AND CONCLUSIONS

Psychologists assume as part of their professional roles a higher duty than that owed by citizens in general to practice their profession in a way that does good and avoids harm. The definition of "good" varies from one application to the next, but clearly psychologists have a moral obligation to embrace cultural diversity in its many forms and, as organizational consultants, to make clear the core values to which they are always committed.

Speaking up about psychologists' core values is often not easy, particularly when corporate or organizational values may be at odds with those of the psychologist. Nonetheless, so long as they are practicing as psychologists, regardless of settings, the obligations remain.

Lefkowitz, in a series of provocative writings (e.g., Lefkowitz, 2003; Lefkowitz & Lowman, 2010), briefly mentioned in Chapter 1 (this volume), takes industrial–organizational psychology (and, by implication, consulting psychology) to task for its often excessive emphasis on corporate values versus those of psychology. He argues that psychologists need to consider how their possible personal alignment with corporate values may affect their commitment to the core values of the profession of psychology.

Of course, psychologists cannot foist their own values onto their organizational clients. But they do have to be sensitive to the values that they as psychologists are required to take seriously and to try to address issues that come up when the two sets of values conflict. In taking on consulting psychology roles, psychologists are doing consulting work for reasons that need to be consistent with the core values of psychology. Increasingly, consulting psychologists are also considering the social justice aspects of their work (see Lowman, 2014), just as corporations are increasingly also considering the impact of their organization on the environment and others who may be affected by its actions. Consulting psychologists can be a force for good in their work with organizations, and at times, they will be the only voice speaking up for human values and cultural diversity. Recognizing the potential conflicts between one's core values as a psychologist and organizational core values can help to assure that discrepant values do not hold too strong a sway over psychologists.

7

Ethical and Professional Standards in the Practice of Consulting Psychology

This is a book about the *professional* practice of consulting psychology. With professionalism come assumptions about the ethics and standards upon which your practice will be based. In this chapter, I focus on ethics and standards as they apply to consulting psychology. Space does not permit a complete treatment of these issues, so I highlight some of the major issues applicable to this field, referring throughout to the American Psychological Association's (APA's; 2010) *Ethical Principles of Psychologists and Code of Conduct* (hereinafter, "Ethics Code").

ETHICAL ISSUES IN THE PRACTICE OF CONSULTING PSYCHOLOGY

The professional practice of psychology in applied settings is complicated enough, and real-life cases raise contingencies that are not always anticipated by the Ethics Code. Consulting psychologists must use judgment to

http://dx.doi.org/10.1037/14853-007
An Introduction to Consulting Psychology: Working With Individuals, Groups, and Organizations,
by R. L. Lowman

apply a broad-brush approach to using the Ethics Code in specific situations (Lowman, 2006). In organizational consulting applications, it is particularly complex to take into account the many different players involved, the respective responsibilities to multiple parties, and the need to anticipate—and to avoid—things that might go wrong.

It was common with earlier versions of the Ethics Code for consulting and organizational psychologists to report that much of the code did not seem very applicable to their work. The 2002 version of the Ethics Code had significant changes for those practicing consulting and organizational psychology, as it incorporated far more explicit references to issues in these fields than any of its predecessor versions.

The efforts to revise the Ethics Code to reflect organizational consulting and organizations and groups were heavily influenced by APA's Division 13 (Society of Consulting Psychology). Representatives from this division attended the sessions held by the group responsible for changes to the Ethics Code. Their goal was to help the Ethics Code be more explicit about how it applies to the practices of psychologists who consult to organizations and groups. This happened not by any radical change but mostly by adding in the recognition that organizations can be clients. As an example, "organizational consulting" was added to the preamble in introducing the applicability of the Ethics Code to psychologists' activities. Similarly, the Ethics Code states:

> Psychologists may disclose confidential information with the appropriate consent of *the organizational client*, the individual client/patient, or another legally authorized person on behalf of the client/patient unless prohibited by law. (Standard 4.05a; emphasis added)

The Ethics Code now has a rather large number of references to "organizations," "organizational clients," "consulting," and "consulting psychology." This contrasts starkly with the numbers of such mentions in prior versions.

Avoiding Harm

In this section, I identify and discuss some of the Standards of the APA Ethics Code and discuss their relevance for the practice of consulting psychology.

Let's start with the fundamental ethical obligation assigned by most professions: to do no harm. Standard 3.04 states this well:

> Psychologists take reasonable steps to avoid harming their clients/ patients, students, supervisees, research participants, organizational clients, and others with whom they work, and to minimize harm where it is foreseeable and unavoidable.

Can consulting psychologists cause harm? The answer to that is certainly yes. They can, for example, misadvise organizations on selection procedures, cause damage to the organization or group by insensitivity to the group's and organization's norms and expectations, miss out on important power dynamics, fail to understand the types of organizations with which they are working, and propose interventions with no (or limited) evidence of validity. They may also coach individuals whose jobs are on the line and act in a way (because of, e.g., their lack of training or understanding of organizational dynamics) that causes incumbents difficulty in retaining their positions.

Case 12: Keeping Promises: Confidentiality of Survey Data

A company's in-house psychologist, as part of his duties, develops and administers an annual employee survey. Each manager who has 10 or more respondents to the survey is to receive a specific report about the employee attitudes of their group or organizational unit. This includes a full report with various scales, means, and standard deviations of the results of the group or unit along with normative data of the results compared with other groups within the organization. The data also include information on what various levels of statistical scores mean, as well as a few special indices the company's psychologists have been developing. The terms of the project had always been that the information was to be used solely for developmental purposes.

A senior manager called a meeting of all the leaders in his area and asked (in an implied command) to see the names and results of all supervisors whose indices were in the bottom third of the organization. He insisted on seeing an action plan for each of the managers in the lowest third and the implication was that they were not to receive raises or performance bonuses until the numbers improved. Those whose numbers did not improve over a 6-month period were to be terminated. However, the manager did not look into some of the possible reasons for low scores. Low scores may have been due to unhappiness with a manager's style or approach, changes in the work unit over which the manager had no control, or new managers in the business unit and needing to make major changes for which resistance would likely be experienced. Each situation would require specific examination to know the sources of the problems.

With the senior manager's action plan (not giving raises or bonuses, the threat of termination), the process suddenly went from being developmental to being punitive. The psychologist raised concerns with the senior manager, advising about why this was a bad idea and was contrary to the identified purposes of the assessment. When the manager would not budge, the managers whose units had low scores became overly solicitous of their employees and being less insistent on performance improvements of their subordinates. Morale of the affected supervisors decreased and several of those rating lower left the organization. The psychologist let the matter drop and assigned the following year's survey to a subordinate.

The creation of psychological measures for evaluating employee attitudes is something psychologists can do very well. But the work of psychologists can be misused, and this case provides such an example. Harm was created by the unintended uses to which the assessment instrument and process were put.

It is never possible for consulting psychologists to anticipate every situation in which harm might be caused. The job of the psychologist is to do the work to professional standards and to seek to minimize harm by anticipating misuses. When, despite the psychologist's best efforts, concerns arise, the psychologist needs to speak up and to do as much as possible to avoid harm to assessees, to the assessment process, and to the organization itself. In the case above, the psychologist did attempt to stop the problematic behavior. Those efforts were unsuccessful. Once the damage had been done, the credibility of the assessment process was in doubt. The psychologist then had the obligation to continue to pursue the concerns with the supervisors of the senior managers if necessary, and to discontinue the program if it was going to be used in a way to cause harm.

Competence

A second fundamental ethical imperative is for psychologists to be competent in their professional work. The relevant Ethical Standard from the APA Ethics Code is the following:

> Psychologists provide services, teach, and conduct research with populations and in areas only within the boundaries of their competence, based on their education, training, supervised experience, consultation, study, or professional experience. (Standard 2.01a)

This Standard creates an unambiguous ethical obligation for psychologists to be competent in whatever they do professionally. They are generally given a great deal of latitude to practice in areas in which they have established their competencies. But judgment requires self-discipline and the willingness to acknowledge what one does not know.

APA Ethical Standard 2.01b, discussed in Chapter 6, extends the need for competence to the area of individual differences, defining multiculturalism as a standard of competence. The next part of the standards relating to competence makes clear that when psychologists extend their work into areas new to them, they seek out relevant training and supervision. It states:

> Psychologists planning to provide services, teach, or conduct research involving populations, areas, techniques, or technologies new to them undertake relevant education, training, supervised experience, consultation, or study. (Standard 2.01c)

This Standard speaks directly to those transitioning to consulting roles from other areas of psychological practice. It suggests the need to seek out proper training and supervision, as well as study, if one has not been trained in consultative roles.

Finally, it might be argued that consulting psychology is still an emerging area of psychological practice, a true statement for some aspects of consulting psychology but not for others. Although in some consulting psychology areas such as assessment the knowledge and practice base are well established and well-integrated into training programs, interventions, however, are often less well researched or what is known may not be widely taught. For example, increasing evidence indicates that coaching, for example (see, e.g., Grant, 2013; Lowman, 2013a), is effective in addressing a number of issues at the individual and team levels, but very few psychology programs incorporate formal training in coaching into their curricula. And considerable research needs to be done before researchers know what works reliably in coaching, what does not, and with which populations. Similarly other aspects of consulting psychology are still emerging as areas of professional practice. Therefore the following APA Ethical Standard is relevant to working in this area:

> In those emerging areas in which generally recognized standards for preparatory training do not yet exist, psychologists nevertheless take reasonable steps to ensure the competence of their work and to protect clients/patients, students, supervisees, research participants, organizational clients, and others from harm. (Standard 2.01e)

Also very important for consulting psychologists' work is Ethical Standard 2.04 which states, "Psychologists' work is based upon established scientific and professional knowledge of the discipline." (See also Standards 2.01e, Boundaries of Competence, and 10.01b, Informed Consent to Therapy.)

Consulting psychologists are, I argue, psychologists first, and consultants second. One of the primary requirements of all of psychologists' work is that it be based on the scientific and professional knowledge of the discipline. This also implies the need for psychologists to be up to date in their knowledge of the literature. Particularly in areas such as organizational and consulting psychology, the knowledge base is rapidly changing, psychologists need to read the journals and books that will update their knowledge and to attend seminars relevant to their areas of expertise. Learning as a professional psychologist is never done.

Informed Consent

As described in the Ethics Code,

> When psychologists conduct research or provide assessment, therapy, counseling, or consulting services in person or via electronic transmission or other forms of communication, they obtain the informed consent of the individual or individuals using language

that is reasonably understandable to that person or persons except when conducting such activities without consent is mandated by law or governmental regulation or as otherwise provided in this Ethics Code. (Standard 3.10a)

Psychologists appropriately document written or oral consent, permission, and assent. (Standard 3.10d)

(See also Standards 8.02, Informed Consent to Research; 9.03, Informed Consent in Assessments; and 10.01, Informed Consent to Therapy.) Not only are there many existing standards addressing issues of informed consent, but also a new Standard was added to the 2002 version of the APA Ethics Code explicitly to address the issues of consulting and organizational psychology:

Psychologists delivering services to or through organizations provide information beforehand to clients and when appropriate those directly affected by the services about (1) the nature and objectives of the services, (2) the intended recipients, (3) which of the individuals are clients, (4) the relationship the psychologist will have with each person and the organization, (5) the probable uses of services provided and information obtained, (6) who will have access to the information, and (7) limits of confidentiality. As soon as feasible, they provide information about the results and conclusions of such services to appropriate persons. (Standard 3.11a)

If psychologists will be precluded by law or by organizational roles from providing such information to particular individuals or groups, they so inform those individuals or groups at the outset of the service. (Standard 3.11b)

This Standard identifies a number of issues that must be addressed in determining who is the client (recognizing that some parties may be clients and others, not) and spells out what needs to be addressed at the start of a consulting relationship. To the extent that these issues have been addressed at the start of a consultative effort, problems down the road are much less likely to occur. Of course, this is not the only Standard of relevance, although it is particularly relevant to issues of informed consent and is thus a good place to start in any client-related activities.

Finally, the Ethics Code has a specific Standard for informed consent in assessments. It states:

> Psychologists obtain informed consent for assessments, evaluations, or diagnostic services, as described in Standard 3.10, Informed Consent, except when (1) testing is mandated by law or governmental regulations; (2) informed consent is implied because testing is conducted as a routine educational, institutional, or organizational activity (e.g., when participants voluntarily agree to assessment when applying for a job); or (3) one purpose of the testing is to evaluate decisional capacity. Informed consent includes an explanation of the nature and purpose of the assessment, fees, involvement of third parties, and limits of confidentiality and sufficient opportunity for the client/patient to ask questions and receive answers. (Standard 9.03a)

Note that this Standard includes an exception for implied consent in testing (in "organizational activity" when, e.g., there is voluntary agreement to participate in employment testing). This does not suggest that in all cases of assessment formal written consent should not be obtained. For example, in conducting executive and other high-stakes executive assessments (e.g., Jeanneret & Silzer, 1998), I prefer to obtain formal written consent so that the people being assessed both know, and have formally agreed to, the assessment procedures. Similarly, I do not always trust that "implied consent" in organizational settings is truly voluntary. Employers tend to take for granted that employees are required to participate in certain developmental activities. Although written consent may not be required, I would still make it a point to inform participants orally and/or in writing of the terms of the engagement as suggested by Ethical Standard 3.11.

Confidentiality

The Ethics Code is very clear on the ethical requirements for psychologists to maintain confidentiality and to protect confidential information. The following Ethical Standard is unambiguous (see also Standard 2.05):

> Psychologists have a primary obligation and take reasonable precautions to protect confidential information obtained through or stored

in any medium, recognizing that the extent and limits of confidentiality may be regulated by law or established by institutional rules or professional or scientific relationship. (Standard 4.01)

However, some limits to confidentiality need to be explained at the beginning of services. This is a complex issue in the practice of consulting psychology. Issues of suicide or homicide risk are generally low in working with clients on work-related concerns, but they are not nonexistent. Psychologists working as consultants may or may not have a legal obligation to breach confidentiality, but prudence dictates that the idea of exceptions to confidentiality be introduced at the beginning of one's work with clients. The Ethics Code addresses this issue as follows:

> Psychologists discuss with persons (including, to the extent feasible, persons who are legally incapable of giving informed consent and their legal representatives) and organizations with whom they establish a scientific or professional relationship (1) the relevant limits of confidentiality and (2) the foreseeable uses of the information generated through their psychological activities. (Standard 4.02a; see also Standard 3.10, Informed Consent)

> Unless it is not feasible or is contraindicated, the discussion of confidentiality occurs at the outset of the relationship and thereafter as new circumstances may warrant. (Standard 4.02b)

> Psychologists who offer services, products, or information via electronic transmission inform clients/patients of the risks to privacy and limits of confidentiality. (Standard 4.02c)

The problem for consulting psychologists is that the assumption cannot be made that they hold a legally protected right to privilege not to disclose confidential information provided by the client in the consultation. Suppose, for instance, an industrial–organizational (I-O) psychologist is not licensed because her state does not permit the licensure of someone with her background and training. She begins work as a psychologist with a coaching client. Suppose that the client discloses a desire to quit his job, is subsequently fired from it, and sues the organization for wrongful discharge. The employer subpoenas the psychologist for a deposition and point blank asks the psychologist whether the client disclosed that he was unhappy in his position and was seeking other employment. Although laws vary from one jurisdiction to another, in many, without licensure there is likely not a legal basis for resisting disclosure. The psychologist can assert that the information is protected by confidentiality, but she may not be able to guarantee that the information will not be required to be disclosed. Clients should know that possibility (even if it may be an unlikely occurrence) before starting work with the psychologist. It is the responsibility of psychologists to know the ground rules and the exceptions both at the beginning of the relationship and over its course. Should unanticipated issues and circumstances affecting confidentiality arise over the course of the intervention they must deal with them at the time they become known.

Multiple Relationships

Psychologists I have trained typically believe that multiple relationships are unethical. The definition of a multiple relationship and the conditions under which they are acceptable is a bit complicated. Here is the relevant APA Ethics Code Standard:

> A multiple relationship occurs when a psychologist is in a professional role with a person and (1) at the same time is in another role with the same person, (2) at the same time is in a relationship with a person closely associated with or related to the person with whom the psychologist has the professional relationship, or (3) promises to enter into another relationship in the future with the person or a person closely associated with or related to the person. A psychologist refrains from entering into a multiple relationship if the multiple relationship could reasonably be expected to impair the psychologist's objectivity, competence, or effectiveness in performing his or her functions as a psychologist, or otherwise risks exploitation or harm to the person with whom the professional relationship exists. Multiple relationships that would not reasonably be expected to cause impairment or risk exploitation or harm are not unethical. (Standard 3.05a)

> If a psychologist finds that, due to unforeseen factors, a potentially harmful multiple relationship has arisen, the psychologist takes

reasonable steps to resolve it with due regard for the best interests of the affected person and maximal compliance with the Ethics Code. (Standard 3.05b)

Many commentators on ethics in consulting psychology, including myself (see Lowman, 2013a), have noted that multiple relationships are the norm, not the exception, in organizational consulting. This is because organizations can be clients, but the consulting psychologist also works with individuals who have reporting relationships to persons in authority and the psychologist has relationships to each. Before agreeing to take on such clients, psychologists must very carefully examine whether these details can be sorted out in a way that acknowledges them and protects against circumstances that would create conflicts of interest.

Examples of multiple relationships in consulting psychology abound. Psychologists who coach individuals while having their organization as a client are in a multiple relationship. Psychologists who work as internal consultants from within an organization who coach persons to whom they directly or indirectly report are in multiple relationships. Those who assess candidates for an organization in which they have responsibilities both to those assessed and the organization paying the costs of the assessments are also in dual relationships. A psychologist consulting to two organizations in competition with another is also in a multiple relationship. And organizations and consulting roles are not static: People change positions and roles over time, and what was not a multiple relationship at one point may become one at another point.

These are normative situations encountered by consulting psychologists. They are not unethical per se, but they do require close attention to the potentially conflicting interests in dealing with multiple individuals. Ethical Standard 3.11 is very helpful in sorting out these roles and determining whether it is appropriate to proceed and when the roles and relationships might need reassessing.

The following are some questions related to multiple relations. The questions are composites of ones that I have been asked over the years by graduate students or professionals in various courses or ethics workshops I have offered.

Question: Is it ethical for a psychologist to provide coaching services to the spouse or the dependent child of her boss?

Answer: Generally, no. To the extent that the coaching services to be provided are intended to be psychological in nature, the role conflicts that could arise with such coaching could lead to knowing personal information about a third party or to meeting with both parties in a way that could affect the primary relationship of the psychologist and the psychologist's boss. Unless one is in an isolated rural area in which there are no other qualified providers within a reasonable geographic distance (and even then it would be important to know why virtual services could not be delivered), it would be best to avoid multiple roles that can reasonably be avoided.

Question: Can one provide psychological services to an employee in an organization and also report back to the employee's supervisor and seek out information from the employee's peers and subordinates?

Answer: Yes, with permission of the identified client and with clearly defined parameters about your role and relationship with each party. Ethical Standard 3.11 is important to consult in this context. It is important for the identified client to give voluntary consent not that in which there is no real choice because the only option to not consenting is, say, termination. This is particularly important when coaching or consulting with individuals whose performance is problematic.

Avoiding Conflicts of Interest

Consulting psychologists must also guard against ethical problems associated with conflicts of interest. The relevant Ethical Standard is the following:

> Psychologists refrain from taking on a professional role when personal, scientific, professional, legal, financial, or other interests or relationships could reasonably be expected to (1) impair their objectivity, competence, or effectiveness in performing their functions as psychologists or (2) expose the person or organization with whom the professional relationship exists to harm or exploitation. (Standard 3.06)

Consulting psychologists may be self-employed or work for other firms, both large and small. Independent practitioners or those in small boutique consulting firms often deliver the services for which they win contracts. For large firms, the marketing techniques and company philosophy may be one of selling as much as possible to each client. Client services sold not because they are particularly necessary for the client but for the primary purpose of building revenues constitute a conflict of interest. Consulting psychologists in a position to recommend assessment measures who utilized their own instruments because the potential markup is higher experience conflicts of interest. Eternal vigilance is needed to avoid placing the consulting psychologists' own needs above those of their clients. By no means are these issues unique to professionals who are psychologists but neither can they be ignored by them even when they may have economic impact for the psychologist's practice.

Assessments

Many psychologists conduct assessments as part of their consulting work. Assessments can be very powerful in identifying dynamics of individuals, groups, and organizations. They can be critically important in understanding what needs to be addressed and in decreasing the time needed between problem identification and effective intervention. But assessments can also be misused, either because they are not appropriate or are not validated for the inferences for which the consulting psychologist is attempting to use them, or because the results are inappropriately fed back to the individuals assessed resulting in potential harm and worsening of performance (see Nowack & Mashihi, 2012). Several relevant Ethical Standards are highlighted below, starting with Standard 9.01 (Bases for Assessments; see also Standards 2.01, 2.04, and 9.06):

(a) Psychologists base the opinions contained in their recommendations, reports, and diagnostic or evaluative statements, including forensic testimony, on information and techniques sufficient to substantiate their findings. (Standard 9.01a)

(b) Except as noted in 9.01c, psychologists provide opinions of the psychological characteristics of individuals only after they have conducted an examination of the individuals adequate to support their statements or conclusions. When, despite reasonable efforts, such an examination is not practical, psychologists document the efforts they made and the result of those efforts, clarify the probable impact of their limited information on the reliability and validity of their opinions, and appropriately limit the nature and extent of their conclusions or recommendations. (Standard 9.01b)

(c) When psychologists conduct a record review or provide consultation or supervision and an individual examination is not warranted or necessary for the opinion, psychologists explain this and the sources of information on which they based their conclusions and recommendations. (Standard 9.01c)

Standard 9.01a establishes the requirement that assessments must be based on "techniques sufficient to substantiate their findings," meaning that care should be taken in drawing conclusions on the basis of limited or insufficient evidence, and Standard 9.01b admonishes psychologists not to draw conclusions on persons they have not examined—important to remember when responding to requests about the behavior of individuals whom the psychologist has not actually assessed.

Case 13: Ethics of Selection

This case concerns a selection assessment conducted by a psychologist involving a number of middle managers for promotion consideration to a senior management position. The hiring official, who was also the client of the psychologist, expressed her preference for a particular candidate she hoped would get the position. She implied that the psychologist would likely receive additional consulting work if the results were in the desired direction. However, another of the candidates performed much better on the assessment than did the preferred candidate.

The APA Ethics Code makes clear that "Psychologists' work is based upon established scientific and professional knowledge of the discipline" (Standard 2.04) and that psychologists base their recommendations on "techniques sufficient to substantiate . . . findings" (Standard 9.01). Neither standard would allow the psychologist, if serving as the decision maker or in making recommendations to the decision maker, to simply void the assessment process by allowing the preferences of the hiring manager to prevail. That would be basing judgments on nonscience-based recommendations (Standard 2.04) and using an approach whose evidence would not be sufficient to justify the conclusions (Standard 9.03). Additionally, if such an approach were based on the imagined future contracts associated with making the desired recommendation, Standard 3.06 (Conflicts of Interest) would also apply.

Although the psychologist would never be justified in ignoring the recommendations of the assessments, assuming that the assessments were job-related, based on appropriate assessment measures, and properly interpreted, the preferences of the hiring manager should not be ignored. Why is it that the manager imagines that the preferred candidate would be more effective in the position? Are there data from actual job performance that provide direct evidence of superior performance? Or does the manager project that the candidate doing well in the assessment might be difficult to work with, or perhaps less tolerant of, political influence? These are all legitimate questions to discuss with the hiring manager, assuming that the psychologist's obligation to honor the results of the assessment had been made clear.

In general, psychological assessments can be powerful predictors of future job behavior. But they are not foolproof. Hiring decisions should be made on the basis of integrating psychological findings with other sources of information, such as the results of employment interviews and actual job performance. However, psychologists have the same obligation as with other predictors to ensure that such information is reliable and valid for the intended inferences (see, e.g., Van Iddekinge, Raymark, & Roth, 2005).

Another possibility to consider is needing to rule out an otherwise well-performing assessment candidate. Predictors of behavior that would be problematic on the job (e.g., lapses of integrity, narcissistic or mercurial behavior) are not predicted by the same variables as are those associated with positive job performance. For example, in one assessment with which I was involved, one of the best-performing candidates was universally resisted by the team of employees who had been selected to make the staffing recommendations. The team was enjoined to identify in great detail the basis of their objections. The evidence was consistent and compelling and pointed to a candidate who not only had very poor social skills but who also was aggressive and direct; for instance, when passing people on the shop floor, not only would he not greet people coming in the opposite direction but he would also intentionally physically bump into them. Additionally, many well-performing candidates threatened that if he were selected for the team, they would not join it.

Because the selection for which the individuals were being considered involved self-directed teams, and because the evidence was sufficiently compelling, consistent, and established to be reliable, it was ultimately determined that the threat to team cohesiveness was sufficiently high to justify the rule-out decision (one that should never be made lightly when the evidence for selection is otherwise very strong). Providing feedback to the nonselected candidate was particularly challenging but also instructive and useful to the unsuccessful candidate.

Consulting psychologists using assessments should be familiar with many provisions within Standard 9, but Standard 9.02 is particularly important. It concerns how and when assessments should be used.

> Psychologists administer, adapt, score, interpret, or use assessment techniques, interviews, tests, or instruments in a manner and for purposes that are appropriate in light of the research on or evidence of the usefulness and proper application of the techniques. (Standard 9.02a)

> Psychologists use assessment instruments whose validity and reliability have been established for use with members of the population tested. When such validity or reliability has not been established, psychologists describe the strengths and limitations of test results and interpretation. (Standard 9.02b)

> Psychologists use assessment methods that are appropriate to an individual's language preference and competence, unless the use of an alternative language is relevant to the assessment issues. (Standard 9.02c)

Standard 9.02a requires that assessment measures be validated for their particular uses and purposes. This implies that assessment projects should begin with asking, "What is the assessment question and which measures are most suited for those inferences?" And not, "What is the test to be used?"

Psychological assessment instruments chosen primarily on the basis of the psychologist's comfort and familiarity with them may or may not match the assessment's purpose—too often they do not. In training thousands of psychologists around the world in assessment methods and having read way too many posts by psychologists to online discussion groups, I am struck by the number of times well-trained psychologists ask the question, "Which tests should I use?" before considering the question, "What psychological characteristics am I trying to measure—and why?" And the questions preceding that one are, "What are the purposes of the assessment? Why is it needed?" and, "What will be done with the results?"

Starting with tests rather than assessment questions can result in a consulting psychology assessment that may be irrelevant—or worse. If it is not likely to cause harm (other than the time and expense, not always trivial, associated with the assessment), neither is it likely to get at the important issues at hand. For example, a widely used measure of personality variables uses an ipsative approach to measurement. It is among the most widely used measures of personality in the world. Knock-offs of it are widely available on the Internet. Yet, from a measurement perspective, the test presents a number of problematic issues (see, e.g., Barbuto, 1997; Pittenger, 2005), whether used as a measure of personality for purposes of selection or development. Or again, a particular verbal reasoning test is widely used by assessors of managerial and leadership candidates, but it is not clear that it is always the best measure to use in all managerial assessment contexts.

Standard 9.02b again raises the question of suitability of assessments for use with particular populations (e.g., men vs. women, ethnic minorities). And Standard 9.02c notes that issues related to language must be considered when an individual's preferred or strongest language is other than the one in which the test is being administered. All of these are very important issues in assessment, but they are a small sliver of the issues needing to be considered in the development and use of assessments, as I discuss in the section below.

STANDARDS OF AND GUIDELINES FOR PROFESSIONAL PRACTICE

Psychologists are covered not just by the Ethics Code but also by various guidelines for practice. These may be specific to a particular area of psychological practice, such as *Record Keeping Guidelines* (APA, 2007b), primarily but not exclusively relevant for health care psychologists, or they can apply to multiple areas of practice, such as the *Guidelines for the Practice of Telepsychology* (hereinafter, Telepsychology Guidelines; Joint Task Force for the Development of Telepsychology Guidelines for Psychologists [Joint Task Force], 2013). In the case of the Telepsychology Guidelines, consulting psychologists conducting a practice that includes video conferencing coaching or assessment, group-level interventions, and even use of the telephone to deliver services will benefit from familiarity with those guidelines. Although the guidelines are not meant to be enforceable in the same way that the Standards of the Ethics Code are, they can still be introduced as evidence in the case of litigation to establish the profession's standards of practice.

Standards for Assessment

It is likely that psychologists working with, in, or through organizations will at one time or another be involved with assessments. The rules and parameters for conducting assessments for purposes of selection, promotion, or performance evaluation are many and complex. Many legal pitfalls can arise when conducting such assessments. At a minimum, consulting psychologists need to have read and to practice with knowledge of the standards, principles, and guidelines described below.

Standards for Educational and Psychological Testing

These standards (American Educational Research Association [AERA], American Psychological Association [APA], & National Council on Measurement in Education [NCME], 2014) constitute the "bible" of testing and are imperative reading for all consulting psychologists using or advising others on the use of psychological assessments. (They are also revised periodically, so psychologists should be sure they are using the current version.) I am often surprised to learn that graduate students in psychology seem more and more rarely to be required to learn even the basic principles of psychometrics. Regardless, psychologists are responsible for professional behavior that is consistent with these guidelines. Read them in small doses if you like but, however you do it, read them in their entirety and consult them in detail as your consulting work takes you in the direction of assessments. Here are some sample standards:

> If the test developer indicates that the conditions of administration are permitted to vary from one test taker or group to another, permissible variation in conditions for administration should be identified. A rationale for permitting the different conditions and any requirements for permitting the different conditions should be documented. (Standard 4.5)

> If evidence based on test content is a primary source of validity evidence supporting the use of a test for selection into a particular job, a similar inference should be made about the test in a new situation only if the job and situation are substantially the same as the job and situation where the original validity evidence was collected. (Standard 11.11; AERA, APA, & NCME, 2014, p. 181)

Principles for the Validation and Use of Personnel Selection Procedures (4th ed.)

The fourth edition of these principles was published by the Society for Industrial and Organizational Psychology [SIOP], (2003). Although these principles (which also are periodically updated) are generally written with test developers in mind they have applicability to test users as well, particularly in using assessments for purposes of selecting candidates for employment or promotion. Consulting psychologists need to understand that all aspects of selection procedures can be the basis for action by relevant governmental groups, such as the Civil Rights Commission. Even the measures used to evaluate employee performance ("the criterion" or outcome measure) are also considered to be tests in the context of applicable laws and guidelines. Below is a sample Principle:

> Measurement bias, namely scores of irrelevant variance that result in systematically higher or lower scores for members of particular groups, is a potential concern for all variables, both predictors and criteria. Determining whether measurement bias is present is often difficult, as this requires comparing an observed score to a true score. In many domains, such as performance appraisal, such a standard is generally unavailable. (C3: SIOP Principles Measurement Bias; SIOP, 2013, p. 33)

Uniform Guidelines on Employee Selection Procedures

Although the Uniform Guidelines on Employee Selection Procedures (hereinafter, Uniform Guidelines; 1978) are nearly 40 years old, they are still relevant and enforced to operationalize and implement the provisions of the Civil Rights Act of 1964 regarding personnel selection. The Uniform Guidelines were subsequently modified as a result of court cases, including those finding their way to the U.S. Supreme Court (see Landy, Guttman, & Outtz, 2010), that provided interpretations of what the Uniform Guidelines required (e.g., the requirement of a job analysis, the technical sufficiency of validation studies, or even what is an appropriate level of statistical significance) and essentially gave them the force of law.

The Uniform Guidelines were intended to be updated over time to reflect new knowledge and understanding. However, the many controversies about the Uniform Guidelines and the larger context in which they are embedded make it unlikely that the U.S. Congress or the Executive Branch will take up the issue anytime soon. Some have argued that they should be revoked (see, e.g., McDaniel, Kepes, & Banks, 2011; Sharf, 2011).

Reading the Uniform Guidelines today, some of what they state is still current. For example:

> B. *Consideration of suitable alternative selection procedures.* Where two or more selection procedures are available which serve the user's

legitimate interest in efficient and trustworthy workmanship, and which are substantially equally valid for a given purpose, the user should use the procedure which has been demonstrated to have the lesser adverse impact. (Uniform Guidelines on Employee Selection Procedures [Uniform Guidelines], 1978, § 1607.3)

However, other aspects are simply outmoded and do not reflect current knowledge. For example:

General standards for validity studies. A. *Acceptable types of validity studies.* For the purposes of satisfying these guidelines, users may rely upon criterion-related validity studies, content validity studies or construct validity studies, in accordance with the standards set forth in the technical standards of these guidelines, section 14 below. New strategies for showing the validity of selection procedures will be evaluated as they become accepted by the psychological profession. (Uniform Guidelines, 1978, § 1607.5)

The Uniform Guidelines cannot be blamed for not incorporating what was not known when they were issued. However, there have been major revolutions in sources of evidence of validity compared to what was available in the 1970s (see, e.g., AERA, APA, & NCME, 2014; Putka & Sackett, 2010; Schmitt, Arnold, & Nieminen, 2010). For example, meta-analyses and validity generalization as an approach to test validation were not contemplated when the Uniform Guidelines were promulgated. And, contrary to the expectation that new strategies for establishing validity would be evaluated, the Uniform Guidelines remain frozen in time because the political will is lacking to make changes in them.

This background is important for consulting psychologists working with selection measures, as they must be able to establish or demonstrate validity of the measures they use for the selection purposes and, when there is adverse impact, they must be prepared to demonstrate that there were not equally valid measures that would have less adverse impact. Knowing the guidelines applicable to personnel selection is an important part of practicing professionally.

Telepsychology Guidelines

It is highly likely, if not inevitable, that consulting psychologists will use electronic media for both assessment and intervention. Unfortunately, psychology licensing laws and other guidelines tend to lag behind the rapidly emerging technological changes. Because consulting psychologists often deal with organizations whose employees are located all over the world, they are frequently called on to consult to individuals and groups in disparate locations. The Telepsychology Guidelines are a good first effort at providing useful instructions for psychologists (Joint Task Force, 2013). Here is how telepsychology is defined in the Telepsychology Guidelines:

> The provision of psychological services using telecommunication technologies. Telecommunications is the preparation, transmission, communication, or related processing of information by electrical, electromagnetic, electromechanical, electro-optical, or electronic means (Committee on National Security Systems, 2010). Telecommunication technologies include but are not limited to telephone, mobile devices, interactive videoconferencing, e-mail, chat, text, and Internet (e.g., self-help websites, blogs, and social media). (Joint Task Force, 2013, p. 791)

In an era of increasing insecurity about information transmitted electronically, consulting psychologists must be particularly careful about the security of electronic transmissions. At the least, clients need to be made aware of the risks. The Telepsychology Guidelines specify:

> Psychologists who provide telepsychology services take reasonable steps to ensure that security measures are in place to protect data and information related to their clients/patients relating to their clients/patients and inform them of the potentially increased risks of loss of confidentiality inherent in the use of the telecommunication technologies, if any. (Guideline 5; Joint Task Force, 2013, p. 797)

For the most part, these guidelines are useful for consulting psychologists in thinking through the issues (e.g., confidentiality, security of electronically transmitted information, and informed consent) with which they need to be concerned. In an era of continual creativity in hacking, even of well-defended information, it can never be assumed that breaches of retained data will not occur. Seeking out communication platforms that are least likely to be breached is part of the psychologist's responsibility. However, consulting psychologists also need to advise clients in advance about potential compromises of presumed confidential information: Be clear that total protection of electronically transmitted data cannot be assured.

OTHER RELEVANT GUIDELINES AND LAWS

The other psychology/professional guidelines with which consulting psychologists need to be familiar include APA's (2003) *Guidelines on Multicultural Education, Training, Research, Practice and Organizational Change for Psychologists* (see Chapter 6, this volume); training guidelines for consulting psychology (APA, 2007b); and for I-O psychology (SIOP, 2003); and guidelines issued from time to time by professional associations about practice or research in specific areas. Laws also change that govern the practice of consulting psychology. Consulting psychologists need to keep current with the rather large amount of guidance, rules, and laws governing the practice of psychology in organizational contexts.

SUMMARY AND CONCLUSIONS

As with many areas of professional psychology practice, consulting psychology is governed by a number of ethical and professional standards. These include the APA Ethics Code, government and professional association principles, and internationally recognized test standards and guidelines. Those practicing in more than one country have other standards and guidelines with which they will have to become familiar. Although these requirements may at times seem onerous, they reflect the advancement of a profession. Over time, more knowledge generates more guidelines and standards. It is a mark of the advancement of the field of psychology in general and consulting psychology in particular that such guidance is available and required learning.

8

The Road Ahead

By now, I hope that it is clear that consulting psychology covers a lot of territory and presents many opportunities for those interested in practicing in this field. Consulting psychology is broader and more complex than one might imagine at first glance. Learning consulting skills is not simply about mastering a few techniques. The foundational skills cut across the domains of individuals, groups, and organizations. I (Lowman, 2002) and the American Psychological Association's (2007a) consulting psychology doctoral training guidelines have argued that the well-trained consulting psychologist must have mastered fundamental competencies in assessment and intervention at the individual, group, and organizational levels. Each of these areas has its own research and professional practice competencies to be learned, not to mention the complex task of integrating across levels.

As the knowledge and skills that comprise the field of consulting psychology broaden and deepen, mastery of specialized knowledge in both

http://dx.doi.org/10.1037/14853-008
An Introduction to Consulting Psychology: Working With Individuals, Groups, and Organizations,
by R. L. Lowman

the practice and research domains will be needed. It is still best to begin one's training learning the fundamentals of the field, which, I argue, will make keeping up with the latest developments easier.

As an analogue, medical students must still learn the names, functions, and structures of the bones in the human body and master the principles of chemistry and biology before obtaining more advanced and specialized knowledge in medicine. Psychology's building blocks are not bones and anatomy but humans and human behavior. As consulting psychologists, people in organizations are our forte. Our first concern is with individual-level characteristics (e.g., interests, abilities, personality) that accompany people when they enter work organizations, because they are most fundamental. These characteristics are also structural (relatively fixed, within a range at least) and highly influential on behavior.

However, consulting contexts are largely social contexts, so it is not enough to know only about human beings as individuals. Groups—with their own structures, functions, and processes—are still the fundamental building blocks of organizations with which consulting psychologists need to be familiar. Similarly, organizations have their own dimensions, vocabulary, power dynamics, and complexities. And all of these are awash in a sea of cultural factors (Gerstein, Heppner, Ægisdóttir, Leung, & Norsworthy, 2009; Glover & Friedman, 2015; Plant, 1950) that envelops behavior and behavioral expectations. As Steward (1972, as cited in Glover & Friedman, 2015) stated it,

> All men eat, but this is an organic and not a cultural fact. It is universally explainable in terms of biological and chemical processes. What and how different groups of men eat is a cultural fact explainable only by culture history and environmental factors. (p. 8)

PATHS TO DEVELOPING CONSULTING PSYCHOLOGY COMPETENCIES

In time, many consulting psychologists will specialize and become more and more expert in narrower and narrower areas. This is probably inevitable because clients are likely to seek assistance from those who are thought to have specialized expertise. But, I argue, those learning to be consulting psychologists should begin with a broad exposure to all aspects of work and, building on this base, later specialize.

I think that psychology graduate students starting from scratch to learn the profession of consulting psychology should first study individuals—typical individuals in a range of careers and working in various types of organizations (e.g., profit, not-for-profit). I think they should learn all that they can about how individuals select their careers, identify and make use of their talents, come to succeed or to be frustrated in various settings, and understand their journeys to make a living and pursue their dreams and passions. Consulting psychology graduate students should also have at least basic knowledge of abnormal behavior and psycho-pathology.

Ideally, they would next observe many different kinds of teams and groups and in a variety of types or organizations. They can then learn how individuals are affected by the groups in which they are embedded and how groups conspire to influence their attitudes and expectations. I would want them to try their hand (with appropriate supervision) in doing group interventions.

Advancing from observation to assessment and intervention, psychologists-in-training would then spend time in organizations. They could visit and learn about a small organization or two over a period of at least a few months, understand the nature of all the moving parts, and then have the opportunity to share with the organization and its leaders what was learned. Next they would spend some time on assignments with larger and more complex organizations, learning how the cultures across such settings differed.

And I would want them to have work experience (including in the lower level service jobs, e.g., fast food). In this manner, they will forever have empathy for the people whose organizational lives their consulting may influence. I would also want them to have served as a manager of something—however small—in which they had responsibility for managing the work of others so they could understand the perspectives and challenges of leadership.

Such a consulting psychologist, combining this kind of supervised experience at all three levels and having had a rigorous graduate training in the theory and practice of the field, would be at a real advantage in understanding people in the context of groups and organizations. They would also have professional self-confidence as they begin their profession.

OTHER PATHS TO MASTERY

In practice, of course, there is not just one way to become a consulting psychologist. Clinical psychologists typically do not learn in their graduate programs about groups, organizations, or leadership—nor the normal (vs. abnormal) range of individuals—but some transition to become excellent consultants. This is particularly the case when they care (or learn to care) about work and organizational issues and, to some extent, can give up a primary focus on the concerns of those with psychological problems. Those coming from training programs in industrial–organizational (I-O) or social psychology training are generally well trained at the organizational and/or group level but lack experience working with individual clients. Organizational psychologists sometimes overly identify with management and the organization. Additional training may be needed working at the individual level. And those having trained mainly in research areas of psychology will have a longer list of competencies to learn.

As for where to obtain additional training, psychologists making transitions from clinical/counseling training and roles will need to find training opportunities and supervised experience working with groups and organizations. This might be done in a university-based postdoctoral program or in a master's program taken postdoctorally in consulting psychology or a related field. The path for I-O psychologists may require a postgraduate supervised internship or work position in which individual-level assessment and intervention skills can be learned. Again, post docs in consulting psychology or even a post doc master's program or certificate programs are organized ways to learn. Self-training, if rigorous, accompanied by supervised experience would be an alternative path. These learning experiences will have different trajectories but the missing skills can be added.

With systematic preparation to fill in the gaps in their initial training and a genuine commitment to the endeavor, a variety of psychologists can become competent and successful in consulting work. Specialization in a particular level or type of consulting activity can proceed to build on the broad and diverse exposure to the fundamentals of the field. In time, the various pieces will fit together and one will have an ever-greater understanding of each of these components and the self-confidence that comes from experience. And, I would hope, each consulting psychologist will have the opportunity to be involved with a number of different types of organizations (e.g., both for-profit and not-for-profit organizations, manufacturing and service companies, schools, and hospitals; see Backer, 2003). This provides the ability to see what is common across different types of organizations and the ways in which they systematically are different. Well-trained and well-experienced consulting psychologists will also have the opportunity to see firsthand, and to work with, the issues that arise at different developmental and life stages of individuals, groups, and organizations. Consulting psychologists at the beginning of their careers face different learning challenges from those in midcareer and from those making the transition to retirement.

YOUR ROAD AHEAD

I have introduced many topics in this book in the attempt to provide a broad overview of the field of consulting psychology. The rather large literature in each of these topics could not be fully examined in this introduction to the field. Indeed, numerous articles and books have been written about even small sections of these chapters. The goal in this book was to introduce readers to the field of consulting psychology, not to make them experts. The aim also has been to help readers know more about what a wide range of interesting and exciting opportunities there are within this field.

As for me, I have yet to find consulting psychology activities that are not provocative and inherently interesting, and are not worth studying, practicing, and writing about. As I look back on the consulting opportunities with which I have been involved over the years, the individuals whose careers I have played a part in helping to shape, the teams I have helped to become more functional, and the organizations for which my consulting efforts have identified problems or that diffused much needed changes in strategic direction and values, I realize that I have been richly blessed. There's something intrinsically rewarding to me about being able to relatively quickly understand the dynamics of a situation and then work with the client to implement a change process. I wish for you the same excitement and opportunities to make a difference in the world through your own consulting psychology work.

References

Alderfer, C. P. (1968). Organizational diagnosis from initial client reactions to a researcher. *Human Organization, 27,* 260–265. http://dx.doi.org/10.17730/humo.27.3.2485860738t13484

Alderfer, C. P. (1987). An intergroup perspective on group dynamics. In J. W. Lorsch (Ed.), *Handbook of organizational behavior* (pp. 190–222). Englewood Cliffs, NJ: Prentice-Hall.

Alderfer, C. P. (1998). Group psychological consulting to organizations: A perspective on history. *Consulting Psychology Journal: Practice and Research, 50,* 67–77. http://dx.doi.org/10.1037/1061-4087.50.2.67

Alderfer, C. P. (2011). *The practice of organizational diagnosis: Theory and methods.* New York, NY: Oxford University Press.

Almeida, P. L., Ahmetoglu, G., & Chamorro-Premuzic, T. (2014). Who wants to be an entrepreneur? The relationship between vocational interests and individual differences in entrepreneurship. *Journal of Career Assessment, 22,* 102–112. http://dx.doi.org/10.1177/1069072713492923

Amabile, T. M., Barsade, S. G., Mueller, J. S., & Staw, B. M. (2005). Affect and creativity at work. *Administrative Science Quarterly, 50,* 367–403. http://dx.doi.org/10.2189/asqu.2005.50.3.367

American Educational Research Association, American Psychological Association, & National Council on Measurement in Education. (2014). *Standards for educational and psychological testing.* Retrieved from http://www.aera.net/Standards14

American Psychological Association. (2003). Guidelines on multicultural education, training, research, practice, and organizational change for psychologists. *American Psychologist, 58,* 377–402.

American Psychological Association. (2007a). Guidelines for education and training at the doctoral and postdoctoral levels in consulting psychology/ organizational consulting psychology. *American Psychologist, 62*, 980–992. http://dx.doi.org/10.1037/0003-066X.62.9.980

American Psychological Association. (2007b). Record keeping guidelines. *American Psychologist, 62*, 993–1004. http://dx.doi.org/10.1037/0003-066X. 62.9.993

American Psychological Association. (2010). *Ethical principles of psychologists and code of conduct (2002, Amended June 1, 2010)*. Retrieved from http://www. apa.org/ethics/code/index.aspx

Amodio, D. M., & Devine, P. G. (2006). Stereotyping and evaluation in implicit race bias: Evidence for independent constructs and unique effects on behavior. *Journal of Personality and Social Psychology, 91*, 652–661. http://dx.doi. org/10.1037/0022-3514.91.4.652

Argyris, C. (1971). *Intervention theory and method*. Reading, MA: Addison-Wesley.

Arredondo, P., & Reinoso, J. (2003). Multicultural competencies in consultation. In D. B. Pope-Davis, H. L. K. Coleman, W. M. Liu, & R. L. Toporek (Eds.), *International handbook of multicultural competencies in counseling and psychology* (pp. 330–346). Thousand Oaks, CA: Sage. http://dx.doi.org/10.4135/ 9781452231693.n21

Arredondo, P., & Rodriguez, V. (2006). Working with contemporary Latino immigrants. *Counseling and Human Development, 38*, 1–12.

Arredondo, P., & Tovar-Blank, Z. G. (2014). Multicultural competencies: A dynamic paradigm for the 21st century. In F. T. L. Leong, L. Comas-Díaz, G. C. Nagayama Hall, V. C. McLoyd, & J. E. Trimble (Eds.), *APA handbook of multicultural psychology: Vol. 2. Applications and training* (pp. 19–34). Washington, DC: American Psychological Association.

Asch, S. E. (1965). Effects of group pressure on the modification and distortion of judgments. In H. Proshansky & B. Seidenberg (Eds.), *Basic studies in social psychology* (pp. 393–401). New York, NY: Holt, Rinehart & Winston. (Original work published 1951)

Backer, T. E. (2003). Consulting psychology as creative problem solving lessons from my first 3 decades. *Consulting Psychology Journal: Practice and Research, 55*, 107–112. http://dx.doi.org/10.1037/1061-4087.55.2.107

Barbuto, J. J., Jr. (1997). A critique of the Myers–Briggs Type Indicator and its operationalization of Carl Jung's psychological types. *Psychological Reports, 80*, 611–625. http://dx.doi.org/10.2466/pr0.1997.80.2.611

Baron, R. A. (2000). Psychological perspectives on entrepreneurship: Cognitive and social factors in entrepreneurs' success. *Current Directions in Psychological Science, 9,* 15–18. http://dx.doi.org/10.1111/1467-8721.00050

Barrick, M. R., Mount, M. K., & Judge, T. A. (2001). Personality and performance at the beginning of the new millennium: What do we know and where do we go next? *International Journal of Selection and Assessment, 9,* 9–30. http://dx.doi.org/10.1111/1468-2389.00160

Barry, B., & Stewart, G. L. (1997). Composition, process, and performance in self-managed groups: The role of personality. *Journal of Applied Psychology, 82,* 62–78. http://dx.doi.org/10.1037/0021-9010.82.1.62

Beck, A. (1981). A study of group phase development and emergent leadership. *Group, 5,* 48–54.

Benz, M., & Frey, B. S. (2008). The value of doing what you like: Evidence from the self-employed in 23 countries. *Journal of Economic Behavior & Organization, 68,* 445–455. http://dx.doi.org/10.1016/j.jebo.2006.10.014

Berry, C. M., Sackett, P. R., & Wiemann, S. (2007). A review of recent developments in integrity test research. *Personnel Psychology, 60,* 271–301. http://dx.doi.org/10.1111/j.1744-6570.2007.00074.x

Binder, J., Brown, R., Zagefka, H., Funke, F., Kessler, T., Mummendey, A., . . . Leyens, J. (2009). Does contact reduce prejudice or does prejudice reduce contact? A longitudinal test of the contact hypothesis among majority and minority groups in three European countries. *Journal of Personality and Social Psychology, 96,* 843–856. http://dx.doi.org/10.1037/a0013470

Blanton, J. S. (2007). In the halls of business: Consulting psychology as a career. In R. J. Sternberg (Ed.), *Career paths in psychology: Where your degree can take you* (2nd ed., pp. 259–278). Washington, DC: American Psychological Association.

Block, J., Sandner, P., & Spiegel, F. (2015). How do risk attitudes differ within the group of entrepreneurs? The role of motivation and procedural utility. *Journal of Small Business Management, 53,* 183–206. http://dx.doi.org/10.1111/jsbm.12060

Boyatzis, R. (1982). *Competent manager: A model for effective performance.* New York, NY: Wiley.

Brock, C. L. (2002). Consulting to for-profit organizations. In R. L. Lowman (Ed.), *Handbook of organizational consulting psychology: A comprehensive guide to theories, skills, and techniques* (pp. 469–492). San Francisco, CA: Jossey-Bass.

Brown, J. B., Ryan, B. L., Thorpe, C., Markle, E. R., Hutchison, B., & Glazier, R. H. (2015). Measuring teamwork in primary care: triangulation of qualitative and quantitative data. *Families, Systems, & Health.* Advance online publication. http://dx.doi.org/10.1037/fsh0000109

Bruyère, S. M., & O'Keeffe, J. (1993). *Implications of the Americans With Disabilities Act for psychology.* New York, NY: Springer.

Burns, J. M. (1956). *Roosevelt: The lion and the fox.* New York, NY: Harcourt Brace.

Burns, J. M. (1960). *John Kennedy: A political profile.* New York, NY: Harcourt Brace.

Busenitz, L. W., & Barney, J. B. (1997). Biases and heuristics in strategic decision making: Differences between entrepreneurs and managers in large organizations: Differences between entrepreneurs and managers in large organizations. *Academy of Management Best Papers Proceedings,* 85–89. (Accession No. 10341736)

Cameron, K. S., & Quinn, R. E. (2011). *Diagnosing and changing organizational culture: Based on the competing values framework* (3rd ed.). San Francisco, CA: Jossey-Bass.

Caro, R. A. (2013). *Lyndon Johnson: The path to power.* New York, NY: Knopf.

Carree, M. A., & Verheul, I. (2012). What makes entrepreneurs happy? Determinants of satisfaction among founders. *Journal of Happiness Studies, 13,* 371–387. http://dx.doi.org/10.1007/s10902-011-9269-3

Carson, A. D. (1998). The integration of interests, aptitudes, and personality traits: A test of Lowman's matrix. *Journal of Career Assessment, 6,* 83–105. http://dx.doi.org/10.1177/106907279800600106

Cavanagh, M. J., & Spence, G. B. (2013). Mindfulness in coaching: Philosophy, psychology or just a useful skill? In J. Passmore, D. B. Peterson, & T. Freire (Eds.), *The Wiley–Blackwell handbook of the psychology of coaching and mentoring* (pp. 112–134). London, England: Wiley–Blackwell.

Church, A. H., & Waclawski, J. (1998). *Designing and using organizational surveys. A seven-step process.* San Francisco, CA: Jossey-Bass.

Civiello, C. L. (2009). Introduction to the special issue on organizational consulting in national security contexts [Special issue]. *Consulting Psychology Journal: Practice and Research, 61*(1), 1–4. http://dx.doi.org/10.1037/a0015099

Civil Rights Act of 1964. Pub. L. No. 88–352, 78 Stat. 241 (1964).

Clifton, D. O. (1999). Guiding principles for growing a company. *The Psychologist-Manager Journal, 3,* 49–56. http://dx.doi.org/10.1037/h0095856

Converse, J. (2009). *Survey research in the United States: Roots and emergence 1890–1960.* Piscataway, NJ: Transaction. (Original work published 1987)

Cooper, S. E. (2012). Introduction to the special issue on international organizational consulting: Consulting psychology goes global [Special issue]. *Consulting Psychology Journal: Practice and Research, 64,* 243–249. http://dx.doi.org/10.1037/a0031584

Cooper, S. E., & Leong, F. T. L. (2008). Introduction to the special issue on culture, race, and ethnicity in organizational consulting psychology. *Consult-*

ing Psychology Journal: Practice and Research, 60, 133–138. http://dx.doi.org/10.1037/0736-9735.60.2.133

Coukos, P. (2012, June 7). *Myth busting the pay gap* [Blog post]. Retrieved from http://social.dol.gov/blog/myth-busting-the-pay-gap/

Covey, S. R. (1989). *The seven habits of highly effective people: Restoring the character ethic.* New York, NY: Simon & Schuster.

Cummings, T. G., & Worley, C. G. (2014). *Organizational change and development* (10th ed.). Stamford, CT: Cengage.

De Geus, A. P. (2002a). *The living company: Habits for survival in a turbulent business environment.* Cambridge, MA: Harvard Business School Press Books.

De Geus, A. P. (2002b). *The living company: Habits for survival in a turbulent business environment* [Excerpt]. Retrieved from http://www.businessweek.com/chapter/degeus.htm

De Meuse, K. P., Marks, M. L., & Dai, G. (2011). Organizational downsizing, mergers and acquisitions, and strategic alliances: Using theory and research to enhance practice. In S. Zedeck (Ed.), *APA handbook of industrial and organizational psychology: Vol. 3. Maintaining, expanding, and contracting the organization* (pp. 729–768). http://dx.doi.org/10.1037/12171-021

Dealberto, M. J. (2007). Why are immigrants at increased risk for psychosis? Vitamin D insufficiency, epigenetic mechanisms, or both? *Medical Hypotheses, 68,* 259–267. http://dx.doi.org/10.1016/j.mehy.2006.07.040

Deming, W. E. (1986). *Out of the crisis.* Cambridge, MA: MIT Press.

Denison, D., Hooijberg, R., Lane, N., & Lief, C. (2011). *Leading culture change in global organizations: Aligning culture and strategy.* San Francisco, CA: Jossey-Bass.

Devine, P. G. (1989). Prejudice and out-group perception. In A. Tesser (Ed.), *Advanced social psychology* (pp. 467–524). Boston, MA: McGraw-Hill.

Diamond, M. A. (2003). Organizational immersion and diagnosis: The work of Harry Levinson. *Organisational & Social Dynamics, 3,* 1–18.

Dickson, W. J., & Roethlisberger, F. J. (1966). *Counseling in an organization: A sequel to the Hawthorne researchers.* Cambridge, MA: Research Division, Graduate School of Business, Harvard University.

Dowd-Eagle, S., & Eagle, J. (2014). Team-based school consultation. In W. P. Erchul & S. M. Sheridan (Eds.), *Handbook of research in school consultation* (2nd ed., pp. 450–472). New York, NY: Routledge.

Drucker, P. (1982). *The practice of management.* New York, NY: HarperBusiness. (Original work published 1954)

Duhigg, C. (2013). *The power of habit: Why we do what we do in life and business.* New York, NY: Random House.

Dyer, W. (2014). *I can see clearly now.* Carlsbad, CA: Hay House.

Edberg, H. (2010). *Leonardo Da Vinci's top six tips for getting things done.* Retrieved from http://www.positivityblog.com/index.php/2010/07/20/leonardo-da-vincis-top-six-tips-for-getting-things-done/

Eddy, P. (1996). Lessons, legends and legacies: Serving the family business. *Journal of Financial Planning, 9,* 76–79.

Eibach, R. P., & Keegan, T. (2006). Free at last? Social dominance, loss aversion, and White and Black Americans' differing assessments of racial progress. *Journal of Personality and Social Psychology, 90,* 453–467. http://dx.doi.org/10.1037/0022-3514.90.3.453

Englert, P., Sommerville, S., & Guenole, N. (2009). Application of the social marketing model to unemployment counseling: A theoretical perspective. *Journal of Employment Counseling, 46,* 107–114. http://dx.doi.org/10.1002/j.2161-1920.2009.tb00073.x

Feldman, D. C., & Bolino, M. C. (2000). Career patterns of the self-employed: Career motivations and career outcomes. *Journal of Small Business Management, 38,* 53–67.

Ferdman, B. M., & Deane, B. R. (2014). *Diversity at work: The practice of inclusion.* San Francisco, CA: Jossey-Bass.

Fiedler, F. E. (2002). Proactive ways to improve leadership performance. In R. L. Lowman (Ed.), *Handbook of organizational consulting psychology: A comprehensive guide to theory, skills, and techniques* (pp. 399–414). San Francisco, CA: Jossey-Bass.

Fiedler, F. E., & Chemers, M. M. (1987). *Improving leadership effectiveness: The leader match concept.* New York, NY: Wiley.

Fields, D. L. (2013). *Taking the measure of work. A guide to validated scales for organizational research and diagnosis.* Thousand Oaks, CA: Sage.

Filho, E., Tenenbaum, G., & Yang, Y. (2015). Cohesion, team mental models, and collective efficacy: Towards an integrated framework of team dynamics in sport. *Journal of Sports Sciences, 33,* 641–653. http://dx.doi.org/10.1080/02640414.2014.957714

Finch, D. M., Edwards, B. D., & Wallace, J. C. (2009). Multistage selection strategies: Simulating the effects on adverse impact and expected performance for various predictor combinations. *Journal of Applied Psychology, 94,* 318–340. http://dx.doi.org/10.1037/a0013775

Forsyth, D. (2009). *Group dynamics.* Boston, MA: Cengage Learning.

Freedman, A. M. (1999). The history of organization development and the NTL institute: What we have learned, forgotten, and rewritten. *The Psychologist-Manager Journal, 3,* 125–141. http://dx.doi.org/10.1037/h0095863

Freedman, A. M., & Leonard, E. S. (2002). Organizational consulting to groups and teams. In R. L. Lowman (Ed.), *Handbook of organizational consulting psychology: A comprehensive guide to theory, skills, and techniques* (pp. 27–53). San Francisco, CA: Jossey-Bass.

Frost, C. F. (1996). *Changing forever: The well-kept secret of America's leading companies.* East Lansing: Michigan State University Press.

Frost, C. F., Wakeley, J. H., & Ruh, R. A. (1974). *The Scanlon Plan for organizational development: Identity, equity, and participation.* East Lansing: Michigan State University Press.

Fulkerson, J. R. (2012). Organizational consulting in international contexts: An integrative perspective. *Consulting Psychology Journal: Practice and Research, 64,* 325–337. http://dx.doi.org/10.1037/a0031663

Furnham, A., Trickey, G., & Hyde, G. (2012). Bright aspects to dark side traits: Dark side traits associated with work success. *Personality and Individual Differences, 52,* 908–913. http://dx.doi.org/10.1016/j.paid.2012.01.025

Gallup, G. H. (1976). Human needs and satisfactions: A global survey. *Public Opinion Quarterly, 40,* 459–467. http://dx.doi.org/10.1086/268332

Gerstein, L., Heppner, P., Ægisdóttir, S., Leung, S., & Norsworthy, K. (Eds.). (2009). *International handbook of cross-cultural counseling: Cultural assumptions and practices worldwide.* Thousand Oaks, CA: Sage.

Glover, J., & Friedman, H. L. (2015). *Transcultural competence. Navigating cultural differences in the global community.* Washington, DC: American Psychological Association. http://dx.doi.org/10.1037/14596-000

Goleman, D. (1998). *Working with emotional intelligence.* New York, NY: Bantam.

Gould, L. J., Stapley, L. F., & Stein, M. (Eds.). (2004). *Experiential learning in organizations: Applications of the Tavistock group relations approach.* London, England: Karnac.

Grabow, K. M. (2002). Recommendations for managing consultants: The view from inside the corporation. In R. L. Lowman (Ed.), *Handbook of organizational consulting psychology: A comprehensive guide to theories, skills, and techniques* (pp. 759–772). San Francisco, CA: Jossey-Bass.

Grant, A. M. (2013). The efficacy of coaching. In J. Passmore, D. B. Peterson, & T. Freire (Eds.), *The psychology of coaching and mentoring* (pp. 15–39). London, England: Wiley–Blackwell.

Greene, R. (1998). *The 48 laws of power.* New York, NY: Penguin.

Gregory, J. B., & Levy, P. E. (2015). *Feedback in organizational consulting.* Washington, DC: American Psychological Association. http://dx.doi.org/10.1037/14619-000

Hackman, J. R. (1987). The design of work teams. In J. W. Lorsch (Ed.), *Handbook of organizational behavior* (pp. 315–342). Englewood Cliffs, NJ: Prentice-Hall.

Hackman, J. R. (Ed.). (1990). *Groups that work and those that don't. Creating conditions for effective teamwork.* San Francisco, CA: Jossey-Bass.

Hackman, J. R. (2002). *Leading teams: Setting the stage for great performances.* Cambridge, MA: Harvard University Business School.

Hackman, J. R., & Wageman, R. (2005). A theory of team coaching. *The Academy of Management Review, 30,* 269–287. http://dx.doi.org/10.5465/AMR.2005.16387885

Halewood, A., & Tribe, R. (2003). What is the prevalence of narcissistic injury among trainee counselling psychologists? *Psychology and Psychotherapy: Theory, Research and Practice, 76,* 87–102. http://dx.doi.org/10.1348/14760830260569274

Halfhill, T. R., Huff, J. W., Johnson, D. A., Ballentine, R. D., & Beyerlein, M. M. (2002). Interventions that work (and some that don't): An executive summary of the organizational change literature. In R. L. Lowman (Ed.), *Handbook of organizational consulting psychology: A comprehensive guide to theories, skills, and techniques* (pp. 619–644). San Francisco, CA: Jossey-Bass.

Haney, C., Banks, C., & Zimbardo, P. (1973). Interpersonal dynamics in a simulated prison. *International Journal of Criminology & Penology, 1,* 69–97.

Hansen, J. C. (2013). A person–environment fit approach to cultivating meaning. In B. J. Dik, Z. S. Byrne, & M. F. Steger (Eds.), *Purpose and meaning in the workplace* (pp. 37–55). Washington, DC: American Psychological Association. http://dx.doi.org/10.1037/14183-003

Harter, J. K., Schmidt, F. L., & Keyes, C. M. (2003). Well-being in the workplace and its relationship to business outcomes: A review of the Gallup studies. In C. M. Keyes & J. Haidt (Eds.), *Flourishing: Positive psychology and the life well-lived* (pp. 205–224). Washington, DC: American Psychological Association. http://dx.doi.org/10.1037/10594-009

Harter, J. K., Schmidt, F. L., Killham, E. A., & Agrawal, S. (2009). Q_{12} *meta-analysis: The relationship between engagement at work and organizational outcomes.* Lincoln, NE: Gallup.

Hartley, D., Roback, H. B., & Abramowitz, S. I. (1976). Deterioration effects in encounter groups. *American Psychologist, 31,* 247–255. http://dx.doi.org/10.1037/0003-066X.31.3.247

Hartung, P. J., Savickas, M. L., & Walsh, W. B. (Eds.). (2015). *APA handbook of career intervention: Vol. 1. Foundations* (pp. 403–417). Washington, DC: American Psychological Association.

Herndon, L. (2013). Why is racial injustice still permitted in the United States? An international human rights perspective on the United States' inadequate compliance with the international convention on the elimination of all forms of racial discrimination. *Wisconsin International Law Journal, 31,* 322–351.

Hogan, J., Hogan, R., & Kaiser, R. B. (2011). Management derailment. In S. Zedeck (Ed.), *APA handbook of industrial and organizational psychology: Vol. 3. Main-*

taining, expanding, and contracting the organization (pp. 555–575). http://dx.doi.org/10.1037/12171-015

Hogan, R. (2006). *Personality and the fate of organizations.* New York, NY: Routledge.

Holland, J. L. (1997). *Making vocational choices: A theory of vocational personalities and work environments* (3rd ed.). Odessa, FL: Psychological Assessment Resources.

Homans, G. (1950). *The human group.* New York, NY: Harcourt, Brace & World.

Hough, L., & Dilchert, S. (2010). Personality: Its measurement and validity for employee selection. In J. L. Farr & N. T. Tippins (Eds.), *Handbook of employee selection* (pp. 299–319). New York, NY: Routledge.

Hough, L., Ones, D. S., & Viswesvaran, C. (1998, April). *Personality correlates of managerial performance constructs.* Poster session presented at the annual conference of the Society for Industrial and Organizational Psychology, Dallas, TX.

Howard, A. (1994). *Diagnosis for organizational change: Methods and models.* New York, NY: Guilford Press.

Howard, A., & Bray, D. W. (1988). *Managerial lives in transition: Advancing age and changing times.* New York, NY: Guilford Press.

Hugg, T. W., Carson, N. M., & Lipgar, R. M. (1993). *Changing group relations: The next twenty-five years in America.* Jupiter, FL: A. K. Rice Institute.

Hunt, E. (2011). *Human intelligence.* New York, NY: Cambridge University Press.

Inceoglu, I., & Bartram, D. (2012). Global leadership: The myth of multicultural competency. *Industrial and Organizational Psychology: Perspectives on Science and Practice, 5,* 216–218. http://dx.doi.org/10.1111/j.1754-9434.2012.01432.x

Jamal, M. (1997). Job stress, satisfaction, and mental health: An empirical examination of self-employed and non-self-employed Canadians. *Journal of Small Business Management, 35,* 48–57.

James, L. R., & McIntyre, H. H. (2010). Situational specificity and validity generalization. In J. L. Farr & N. T. Tippins (Eds.), *Handbook of employee selection* (pp. 909–920). New York, NY: Routledge.

Jeanneret, R., & Silzer, R. (Eds.). (1998). *Individual psychological assessment: Predicting behavior in organizational settings.* San Francisco, CA: Jossey-Bass.

Johnson, D. A., Beyerlein, M. M., Huff, J. W., Halfhill, T. R., & Ballentine, R. D. (2002). Successfully implementing teams in organizations. In R. L. Lowman (Ed.), *Handbook of organizational consulting psychology: A comprehensive guide to theory, skills, and techniques* (pp. 235–259). San Francisco, CA: Jossey-Bass.

Johnson, J. W., & Oswald, F. L. (2010). Test administration and the use of test scores. In J. L. Farr & N. T. Tippins (Eds.), *Handbook of employee selection* (pp. 151–169). New York, NY: Routledge.

Johnson, S. K. (2008). I second that emotion: Effects of emotional contagion and affect at work on leader and follower outcomes. *The Leadership Quarterly, 19,* 1–19. http://dx.doi.org/10.1016/j.leaqua.2007.12.001

Joint Task Force for the Development of Telepsychology Guidelines for Psychologists. (2013). Guidelines for the practice of telepsychology. *American Psychologist, 68,* 791–800. http://dx.doi.org/10.1037/a0035001

Jones, G., & Spooner, K. (2006). Coaching high achievers. *Consulting Psychology Journal: Practice and Research, 58,* 40–50. http://dx.doi.org/10.1037/1065-9293.58.1.40

Judge, T. A., Bono, J. E., Ilies, R., & Gerhardt, M. W. (2002). Personality and leadership: A qualitative and quantitative review. *Journal of Applied Psychology, 87,* 765–780. http://dx.doi.org/10.1037/0021-9010.87.4.765

Judge, T. A., Piccolo, R. F., & Kosalka, T. (2009). The bright and dark sides of leader traits: A review and theoretical extension of the leader trait paradigm. *The Leadership Quarterly, 20,* 855–875. http://dx.doi.org/10.1016/j.leaqua.2009.09.004

Kaiser, R. B., Hogan, R., & Craig, S. B. (2008). Leadership and the fate of organizations. *American Psychologist, 63,* 96–110. http://dx.doi.org/10.1037/0003-066X.63.2.96

Kaiser, R. B., LeBreton, J. M., & Hogan, J. (2015). The dark side of personality and extreme leader behavior. *Applied Psychology: An International Review, 64,* 55–92. http://dx.doi.org/10.1111/apps.12024

Kalantari, B. (2012). The influence of social values and childhood socialization on occupational gender segregation and wage disparity. *Public Personnel Management, 41,* 241–255.

Kampa-Kokesch, S., & Anderson, M. Z. (2001). Executive coaching: A comprehensive review of the literature. *Consulting Psychology Journal: Practice and Research, 53,* 205–228. http://dx.doi.org/10.1037/1061-4087.53.4.205

Kaslow, F. W. (Ed.). (2006). *Handbook of family business and family business consultation: A global perspective.* New York, NY: International Business Press.

Katz, D., & Kahn, R. L. (1966). *The social psychology of organizations.* New York, NY: Wiley.

Katz, D., & Kahn, R. L. (1978). *The social psychology of organizations* (2nd ed.). New York, NY: Wiley.

Kiatpongsan, S., & Norton, M. I. (2014). How much (more) should CEOs make? A universal desire for more equal pay. *Perspectives on Psychological Science, 9,* 587–593. http://dx.doi.org/10.1177/1745691614549773

Kilburg, R. R. (2000). *Executive coaching: Developing executive wisdom in a world of chaos.* Washington, DC: American Psychological Association. http://dx.doi.org/10.1037/10355-000

Kilburg, R. R. (2007a). Toward a conceptual understanding and definition of executive coaching. In R. R. Kilburg & R. C. Diedrich (Eds.), *The wisdom of coaching: Essential papers in consulting psychology for a world of change* (pp. 21–30). Washington, DC: American Psychological Association. http://dx.doi.org/10.1037/11570-001

Kilburg, R. R. (2007b). When shadows fall: Using psychodynamic approaches in executive coaching. In R. R. Kilburg & R. C. Diedrich (Eds.), *The wisdom of coaching: Essential papers in consulting psychology for a world of change* (pp. 185–205). Washington, DC: American Psychological Association. http://dx.doi.org/10.1037/11570-019

Kines, P., Andersen, L. P. S., Spangenberg, S., Mikkelsen, K. L., Dyreborg, J., & Zohar, D. (2010). Improving construction site safety through leader-based verbal safety communication. *Journal of Safety Research, 41,* 399–406. http://dx.doi.org/10.1016/j.jsr.2010.06.005

King, D., Dalton, D., Daily, C., & Covin, J. (2004). Meta-analyses of post-acquisition performance: Indications of unidentified moderators. *Strategic Management Journal, 25,* 187–200. http://dx.doi.org/10.1002/smj.371

Kolev, G. I. (2008). The stock market bubble, shareholders' attribution bias and excessive top CEO pay. *Journal of Behavioral Finance, 9,* 62–71. http://dx.doi.org/10.1080/15427560802093647

Konnikova, M. (2014, July 22). Getting over procrastination. *New Yorker.* Retrieved from http://www.newyorker.com/science/maria-konnikova/a-procrastination-gene

Korte, R., & Lin, S. (2013). Getting on board: Organizational socialization and the contribution of social capital. *Human Relations, 66,* 407–428. http://dx.doi.org/10.1177/0018726712461927

Kozusznik, M. W., Rodríguez, I., & Peiró, J. M. (2015). Eustress and distress climates in teams: Patterns and outcomes. *International Journal of Stress Management, 22,* 1–23. http://dx.doi.org/10.1037/a0038581

Krause, D. E., Kersting, M., Heggestad, E. D., & Thornton, G. I., III. (2006). Incremental validity of assessment center ratings over cognitive ability tests: A study at the executive management level. *International Journal of Selection and Assessment, 14,* 360–371. http://dx.doi.org/10.1111/j.1468-2389.2006.00357.x

Krueger, N. F. (2007). What lies beneath? The experiential essence of entrepreneurial thinking. *Entrepreneurship Theory and Practice, 31,* 123–138.

Kuba, S. A. (2013). Sexually and gender-variant individuals: International and multicultural perspectives. In R. L. Lowman (Ed.), *Internationalizing multiculturalism: Expanding professional competencies in a globalized world* (pp. 109–142). Washington, DC: American Psychological Association. http://dx.doi.org/10.1037/14044-005

Kulish, N., & Clark, N. (2015, April 18). Germanwings crash exposes history of denial on risk of pilot suicide. *The New York Times.* Retrieved from http://www.nytimes.com/2015/04/19/world/europe/germanwings-plane-crash-andreas-lubitz-lufthansa-pilot-suicide.html?_r=0

Landy, F. J., Guttman, A., & Outtz, J. L. (2010). A sampler of legal principles in employment selection. In J. L. Farr & N. T. Tippins (Eds.), *Handbook of employee selection* (pp. 627–650). New York, NY: Psychology Press.

Leach, M. M., Leong, F. L., Inman, A., & Ciftçi, A. (2013). National origin, national values, and cultural congruence. In R. L. Lowman (Ed.), *Internationalizing multiculturalism: Expanding professional competencies in a globalized world* (pp. 83–107). Washington, DC: American Psychological Association. http://dx.doi.org/10.1037/14044-004

Lefkowitz, J. (2003). *Ethics and values in industrial and organizational psychology.* New York, NY: Erlbaum.

Lefkowitz, J., & Lowman, R. L. (2010). Ethics of employee selection. In J. L. Farr & N. T. Tippins (Eds.), *Handbook of employee selection* (pp. 571–590). New York, NY: Psychology Press.

Leonard, H. S., & Freedman, A. M. (2000). From scientific management through fun and games to high-performing teams: A historical perspective on consulting to team-based organizations. *Consulting Psychology Journal: Practice and Research, 52,* 3–19. http://dx.doi.org/10.1037/1061-4087.52.1.3

Lepsinger, R., & Lucia, A. (2009). *The art and science of 360-degree feedback* (2nd ed.). San Francisco, CA: Wiley.

Levin, I. M. (2002). Consulting with healthcare organizations. In R. L. Lowman (Ed.), *Handbook of organizational consulting psychology: A comprehensive guide to theories, skills, and techniques* (pp. 562–587). San Francisco, CA: Jossey-Bass.

Levinson, H. (with Spohn, A. G., & Molinari, J.). (1972). *Organizational diagnosis.* Cambridge, MA: Harvard University Press.

Levinson, H. (2002a). Assessing organizations. In R. L. Lowman (Ed.), *Handbook of organizational consulting psychology: A comprehensive guide to theories, skills, and techniques* (pp. 315–343). San Francisco, CA: Jossey-Bass.

Levinson, H. (2002b). *Organizational assessment: A step-by-step guide to effective consulting.* Washington, DC: American Psychological Association. http://dx.doi.org/10.1037/10453-000

Levinson, H. (2002c). Psychological consultation to organizations: Linking assessment and intervention. In R. L. Lowman (Ed.), *Handbook of organizational consulting psychology: A comprehensive guide to theories, skills, and techniques* (pp. 415–450). San Francisco, CA: Jossey-Bass.

Levinson, H. (2009). Why the behemoths fell: Psychological roots of corporate failure. In A. M. Freedman & K. H. Bradt (Eds.), *Consulting psychology:*

Selected articles by Harry Levinson (pp. 79–97). Washington, DC: American Psychological Association. http://dx.doi.org/10.1037/11848-006

Levy, P. E., & Williams, J. R. (2004). The social context of performance appraisal: A review and framework for the future. *Journal of Management, 30,* 881–905. http://dx.doi.org/10.1016/j.jm.2004.06.005

Lewin, K. (1946). Behavior and development as a function of the total situation. In L. Carmichael (Ed.), *Manual of child psychology* (pp. 791–844). New York, NY: Wiley. http://dx.doi.org/10.1037/10756-016

Lewin, K. (1948). Group processes and social change. In T. M. Newcomb & E. L. Hartley (Eds.), *Readings in social psychology* (pp. 330–341). New York, NY: Henry Holt.

Lewin, K. (1951). *Field theory in social science.* New York, NY: Harper.

Likert, R. (1961). *New patterns of management.* New York, NY: McGraw-Hill.

Likert, R. (1967). *The human organization: Its management and value.* New York, NY: McGraw-Hill.

Limberg, B. (2013). Religion, spirituality and secularism in multicultural and international contexts. In R. L. Lowman (Ed.), *Internationalizing multiculturalism: Expanding professional competencies in a globalized world* (pp. 143–170). Washington, DC: American Psychological Association. http://dx.doi.org/10.1037/14044-006

Lopez, P. D., & Ensari, N. (2013). Fostering multiculturally and internationally competent groups and teams. In R. L. Lowman (Ed.), *Internationalizing multiculturalism: Expanding professional competencies in a globalized world* (pp. 173–198). Washington, DC: American Psychological Association. http://dx.doi.org/10.1037/14044-007

Low, M. B., & MacMillan, I. C. (1988). Entrepreneurship: Past research and future challenges. *Journal of Management, 14,* 139–161. http://dx.doi.org/10.1177/014920638801400202

Lowe, R. A., & Ziedonis, A. A. (2006). Overoptimism and the performance of entrepreneurial firms. *Management Science, 52,* 173–186. http://dx.doi.org/10.1287/mnsc.1050.0482

Lowman, R. L. (1989). *Pre-employment screening for psychopathology: A guide to professional practice.* Sarasota, FL: Professional Resource Exchange.

Lowman, R. L. (1991). *The clinical practice of career assessment: Interests, abilities, and personality.* Washington, DC: American Psychological Association. http://dx.doi.org/10.1037/10091-000

Lowman, R. L. (1993a). *Counseling and psychotherapy of work dysfunctions.* Washington, DC: American Psychological Association. http://dx.doi.org/10.1037/10133-000

Lowman, R. L. (1993b). The inter-domain model of career assessment and counseling. *Journal of Counseling & Development, 71,* 549–554. http://dx.doi.org/10.1002/j.1556-6676.1993.tb02240.x

Lowman, R. L. (Ed.). (2002). *Handbook of organizational consulting psychology: A comprehensive guide to theories, skills, and techniques.* San Francisco, CA: Jossey-Bass.

Lowman, R. L. (2004). Donald O. Clifton (1924–2003). *American Psychologist, 59,* 180. http://dx.doi.org/10.1037/0003-066X.59.3.180

Lowman, R. L. (2005). Importance of diagnosis in organizational assessment: Harry Levinson's contributions. *The Psychologist-Manager Journal, 8,* 17–28. http://dx.doi.org/10.1207/s15503461tpmj0801_3

Lowman, R. L. (Ed.). (2006). *The ethical practice of psychology in organizations* (2nd ed.). Washington, DC: American Psychological Association, & Society for Industrial and Organizational Psychology. http://dx.doi.org/10.1037/11386-000

Lowman, R. L. (2007). Executive coaching: The road to Dodoville needs paving with more than good assumptions. In R. R. Kilburg & R. C. Diedrich (Eds.), *The wisdom of coaching. Essential papers in consulting psychology for a world of change* (pp. 73–78). Washington, DC: American Psychological Association. http://dx.doi.org/10.1037/11570-007

Lowman, R. L. (2012). Frontier no more: International consulting skills as necessary minimal competencies for consulting psychologists. *Consulting Psychology Journal: Practice and Research, 64,* 338–343. http://dx.doi.org/10.1037/a0031676

Lowman, R. L. (2013a). Coaching ethics. In J. Passmore, D. Peterson, & T. Freire (Eds.), *The Wiley–Blackwell handbook of the psychology of coaching and mentoring* (pp. 68–88). Oxford, England: Wiley–Blackwell.

Lowman, R. L. (Ed.). (2013b). *Internationalizing multiculturalism: Expanding professional competencies in a globalized world.* Washington, DC: American Psychological Association. http://dx.doi.org/10.1037/14044-000

Lowman, R. L. (2014). Social justice in industrial-organizational and consulting psychology. In C. V. Johnson & H. L. Friedman (Eds.), *Praeger handbook of social justice and psychology: Vol. 3. Youth and disciplines* (pp. 165–181). New York, NY: Psychology Press/Routledge.

Lowman, R. L. (2015). *Group observation assignment* [Unpublished course document]. San Diego, CA: Organizational Psychology Program, CSPP/Alliant International University.

Lowman, R. L., & Carson, A. D. (2003). Assessment of interests. In J. R. Graham & J. A. Naglieri (Eds.), *Handbook of psychology: Vol. 10. Assessment psychology* (pp. 467–485). New York, NY: Wiley.

Lowman, R. L., & Carson, A. D. (2012). Conceptualization and assessment of interests. In J. R. Graham & J. A. Naglieri (Eds.), *Handbook of psychology: Vol. 10. Assessment psychology* (2nd ed., pp. 534–557). New York, NY: Wiley. http://dx.doi.org/10.1002/9781118133880.hop210020

Lowman, R. L., Diamond, M. A., & Kilburg, R. R. (2012). Harry Levinson (1922–2012). *American Psychologist, 67,* 800. http://dx.doi.org/10.1037/a0030225

Lowman, R. L., & Ng, Y.-M. (2010). Interest, ability and personality characteristics of two samples of employed realistic males: Implications for management and assessment. *The Psychologist-Manager Journal, 13,* 147–163. http://dx.doi.org/10.1080/10887156.2010.500259

Lubit, R. (2002). The long-term organizational impact of destructively narcissistic managers. *The Academy of Management Executive, 16,* 127–138. http://dx.doi.org/10.5465/AME.2002.6640218

Maccoby, M. (2004). Narcissistic leaders: The incredible pros, the inevitable cons. *Harvard Business Review, 82,* 92–101.

Malos, S. (2012). Employment discrimination based on immigration status: Recent cases involving H-1B visas. *Employee Responsibilities and Rights Journal, 24,* 23–36.

March, J. G., & Simon, H. A. (1993). *Organizations* (2nd ed.). Cambridge, MA: Blackwell. (Original work published 1958)

Marks, M. L., & Mirvis, P. H. (2012). Applying OD to make mergers and acquisitions work. *OD Practitioner, 44,* 5–12.

Mathieu, C., & St-Jean, É. (2013). Entrepreneurial personality: The role of narcissism. *Personality and Individual Differences, 55,* 527–531. http://dx.doi.org/10.1016/j.paid.2013.04.026

Mayer, J. D., Salovey, P., & Caruso, D. R. (2008). Emotional intelligence: New ability or eclectic traits? *American Psychologist, 63,* 503–517. http://dx.doi.org/10.1037/0003-066X.63.6.503

McClelland, D. C., & Burnham, D. H. (2003). Power is the great motivator. *Harvard Business Review.* Retrieved from https://hbr.org/2003/01/power-is-the-great-motivator (Original work published 1976)

McDaniel, M. A., Kepes, S., & Banks, G. C. (2011). The *Uniform Guidelines* are a detriment to the field of personnel selection. *Industrial and Organizational Psychology: Perspectives on Science and Practice, 4,* 494–514. http://dx.doi.org/10.1111/j.1754-9434.2011.01382.x

McIlveen, P. (2015). Psychotherapy, counseling, and career counseling. In P. J. Hartung, M. L. Savickas, W. B. Walsh (Eds.), *APA handbook of career intervention: Vol. 1. Foundations* (pp. 403–417). Washington, DC: American Psychological Association. http://dx.doi.org/10.1037/14438-022

Mechanic, D. (2012). Seizing opportunities under the Affordable Care Act for transforming the mental and behavioral health system. *Health Affairs, 31,* 376–382. http://dx.doi.org/10.1377/hlthaff.2011.0623

Meyer, H. H. (1970). The validity of the in-basket test as a measure of managerial performance. *Personnel Psychology, 23,* 297–307. http://dx.doi.org/10.1111/j.1744-6570.1970.tb01657.x

Miller, A. (1981). *The drama of being a child.* London, England: Virago.

Miller, W. R., Yahne, C. E., Moyers, T. B., Martinez, J., & Pirritano, M. (2004). A randomized trial of methods to help clinicians learn motivational interviewing. *Journal of Consulting and Clinical Psychology, 72,* 1050–1062. http://dx.doi.org/10.1037/0022-006X.72.6.1050

Minbashian, A., Bright, J. H., & Bird, K. D. (2009). Complexity in the relationships among the subdimensions of extraversion and job performance in managerial occupations. *Journal of Occupational and Organizational Psychology, 82,* 537–549. http://dx.doi.org/10.1348/096317908X371097

Mohammed, S., Cannon-Bowers, J., & Foo, S. C. (2010). Selection for team membership: A contingency and multilevel perspective. In J. L. Farr & N. T. Tippins (Eds.), *Handbook of employee selection* (pp. 801–822). New York, NY: Routledge.

Moore, B. F., & Ross, T. L. (1978). *The Scanlon way to improved productivity: A practical guide.* New York, NY: Wiley.

Morrison, K. R., Fast, N. J., & Ybarra, O. (2009). Group status, perceptions of threat, and support for social inequality. *Journal of Experimental Social Psychology, 45,* 204–210. http://dx.doi.org/10.1016/j.jesp.2008.09.004

Newcomb, T. M. (1943). *Personality and social change.* New York, NY: Dryden.

Nowack, K., & Mashihi, S. (2012). Evidence-based answers to 15 questions about leveraging 360-degree feedback. *Consulting Psychology Journal: Practice and Research, 64,* 157–182. http://dx.doi.org/10.1037/a0030011

Nye, C. D., Su, R., Rounds, J., & Drasgow, F. (2012). Vocational interests and performance: A quantitative summary of over 60 years of research. *Perspectives on Psychological Science, 7,* 384–403. http://dx.doi.org/10.1177/1745691612449021

O'Keeffe, J. (Ed.). (1993). Implications of the ADA of 1990 for psychologists [Special issue]. *Consulting Psychology Journal: Practice and Research, 45*(2).

Olkin, R. (2002). Could you hold the door for me? Including disability in diversity. *Cultural Diversity and Ethnic Minority Psychology, 8,* 130–137. http://dx.doi.org/10.1037/1099-9809.8.2.130

Ones, D. S., Dilchert, S., Viswesvaran, C., & Judge, T. A. (2007). In support of personality assessment in organizational settings. *Personnel Psychology, 60,* 995–1027. http://dx.doi.org/10.1111/j.1744-6570.2007.00099.x

Ones, D. S., Dilchert, S., Viswesvaran, C., & Salgado, J. F. (2010). Cognitive abilities. In J. L. Farr & N. T. Tippins (Eds.), *Handbook of employee selection* (pp. 255–275). New York, NY: Routledge.

O*NET. (n.d.-a). *Details report for: 11-1021.001—General and operations managers.* Retrieved from http://www.onetonline.org/link/details/11-1021.00#Interests

O*NET. (n.d.-b). *O*NET online.* Retrieved from http://www.onetonline.org/

O*NET. (n.d.-c). *Quick search for: Psychologist.* Retrieved from http://www.onetonline.org/find/quick?s=psychologist

O*NET. (n.d.-d). *Summary report for 29-1066.00—psychiatrists.* Retrieved from http://www.onetonline.org/link/summary/29-1066.00

Oswald, F. L., & Hough, L. M. (2011). Personality and its assessment in organizations: Theoretical and empirical developments. In S. Zedeck (Ed.), *APA handbook of industrial and organizational psychology: Vol. 2. Selecting and developing members for the organization* (pp. 153–184). http://dx.doi.org/10.1037/12170-005

Palmore, S., & Williams, H. (2013). Cognitive behavioral approaches. In J. Passmore, D. B. Peterson, & T. Freire (Eds.), *The Wiley–Blackwell handbook of the psychology of coaching and mentoring* (pp. 298–318). London, England: Wiley–Blackwell.

Patient Protection and Affordable Care Act. Pub. L. No. 111–148. (2010).

Pearlman, K., & Sanchez, J. I. (2010). Work analysis. In J. L. Farr & N. T. Tippins (Eds.), *Handbook of employee selection* (pp. 73–98). New York, NY: Routledge.

Peltier, B. (2009). *The psychology of executive coaching: Theory and application* (2nd ed.). New York, NY: Routledge.

Peterson, D. B. (2011). Executive coaching: A critical review and recommendations for advancing the practice. In S. Zedeck (Ed.), *APA handbook of industrial and organizational psychology: Vol. 2. Selecting and developing members for the organization* (pp. 527–566). http://dx.doi.org/10.1037/12170-018

Pittenger, D. (2005). Cautionary comments regarding the Myers–Briggs Type Indicator. *Consulting Psychology Journal: Practice and Research, 57,* 210–221. http://dx.doi.org/10.1037/1065-9293.57.3.210

Plant, J. S. (1950). *The envelope: A study of the impact of the world upon the child.* Oxford, England: Commonwealth Fund. http://dx.doi.org/10.4159/harvard.9780674421516

Prien, E. P., Schippmann, J. S., & Prien, K. O. (2003). *Individual assessment as practiced industry and consulting.* Mahwah, NJ: Erlbaum.

Pryor, R. G., & Ward, R. T. (1985). Unemployment: What counselors can do about it. *Journal of Employment Counseling, 22,* 3–17. http://dx.doi.org/10.1002/j.2161-1920.1985.tb00807.x

Purvanova, R. K. (2014). Face-to-face versus virtual teams: What have we really learned? *The Psychologist-Manager Journal, 17,* 2–29. http://dx.doi.org/10.1037/mgr0000009

Putka, D. J., & Sackett, P. R. (2010). Reliability and validity. In J. L. Farr & N. T. Tippins (Eds.), *Handbook of employee selection* (pp. 9–49). New York, NY: Routledge.

Randahl, G. J. (1991). A typological analysis of the relations between measured vocational interests and abilities. *Journal of Vocational Behavior, 38,* 333–350. http://dx.doi.org/10.1016/0001-8791(91)90034-J

Roberts, B. W., Chernyshenko, O. S., Starks, S., & Goldberg, L. R. (2005). The structure of conscientiousness: An empirical investigation based on seven major personality questionnaires. *Personnel Psychology, 58,* 103–139.

Roethlisberger, F. J., & Dickson, W. J. (1939). *Management and the worker.* Cambridge, MA: Harvard University Press.

Rosenfield, S. J., & Humphrey, C. F. (Eds.). (2012). Consulting psychology in education: Challenge and change [Special issue]. *Consulting Psychology Journal: Practice and Research, 64*(1). http://dx.doi.org/10.1037/a0027825

Sandhu, D. S. (2002). *Counseling employees: A multifaceted approach.* Alexandria, VA: American Counseling Association.

Sashkin, M. (1982). Interview. *Group & Organization Studies, 7,* 135–162.

Savickas, M. L. (2011). *Career counseling.* Washington, DC: American Psychological Association.

Schein, E. H. (1998). *Process consultation revisited. Building the helping relationship.* Englewood Cliffs, NJ: Prentice-Hall.

Schein, E. H. (2009). *Helping: How to offer, give, and receive help.* San Francisco, CA: Barrett-Kohler.

Schein, E. H. (2010). *Organizational culture and leadership* (4th ed.). San Francisco, CA: Barrett-Kohler.

Schein, E. H. (2013). *Humble inquiry: The gentle art of asking instead of telling.* San Francisco, CA: Barrett-Kohler.

Schmidt, F. L. (2002). The role of general cognitive ability and job performance: Why there can be no debate. *Human Performance, 15,* 187–210. http://dx.doi.org/10.1080/08959285.2002.9668091

Schmidt, F. L. (2014). A general theoretical integrative model of individual differences in interests, abilities, personality traits, and academic and occupational achievement: A commentary on four recent articles. *Perspectives on Psychological Science, 9,* 211–218. http://dx.doi.org/10.1177/1745691613518074

Schmidt, F. L., & Hunter, J. (2004). General mental ability in the world of work: Occupational attainment and job performance. *Journal of Personality and Social Psychology, 86,* 162–173. http://dx.doi.org/10.1037/0022-3514.86.1.162

Schmitt, N. W. (2014). Personality and cognitive ability as predictors of effective performance at work. *Annual Review of Organizational Psychology and Organizational Behavior, 1,* 45–65.

Schmitt, N. W., Arnold, J. D., & Nieminen, L. (2010). Validation strategies for primary studies. In J. L. Farr & N. T. Tippins (Eds.), *Handbook of employee selection* (pp. 51–71). New York, NY: Routledge.

Seong, J. Y., Kristof-Brown, A. L., Park, W.-W., Hong, D.-S., & Shin, Y. (2015). Person–group fit: Diversity antecedents, proximal outcomes, and performance at the group level. *Journal of Management, 41,* 1184–1213.

Sharf, J. C. (2011). Equal employment versus equal opportunity: A naked political agenda covered by a scientific fig leaf. *Industrial and Organizational Psychology: Perspectives on Science and Practice, 4,* 537–539. http://dx.doi.org/10.1111/j.1754-9434.2011.01387.x

Shaw, M. E. (1971). *Group dynamics: The psychology of small group behavior.* New York, NY: McGraw-Hill.

Sherif, M., & Sherif, C. (1958). *An outline of social psychology.* Oxford, England: Harper.

Sherin, J., & Caiger, L. (2004). Rational-emotive behavior therapy: A behavioral change model for executive coaching. *Consulting Psychology Journal: Practice and Research, 56,* 225–223. http://dx.doi.org/10.1037/1065-9293.56.4.225

Sims, C. M. (2014). Self-regulation coaching to alleviate student procrastination: Addressing the likeability of studying behaviours. *International Coaching Psychology Review, 9,* 147–164.

Smith, M. L., & Glass, G. V. (1977). Meta-analysis of psychotherapy outcome studies. *American Psychologist, 32,* 752–760. http://dx.doi.org/10.1037/0003-066X.32.9.752

Society for Industrial and Organizational Psychology. (2003). *Principles for the validation and use of personnel selection procedures* (4th ed.). Bowling Green, OH: Author. Retrieved from http://www.siop.org/_Principles/principles.pdf

Spence, G. B., Cavanagh, M. J., & Grant, A. M. (2008). The integration of mindfulness training and health coaching: An exploratory study. *Coaching: An International Journal of Theory, Research and Practice, 1,* 145–163. http://dx.doi.org/10.1080/17521880802328178

Srinivasan, A., & Kurey, B. (2014). Creating a culture of quality. *Harvard Business Review, 92,* 23–25.

Stelter, R. (2014). Third-generation coaching: Reconstructing dialogues through collaborative practice and a focus on values. *International Coaching Psychology Review, 9,* 51–66.

Sternberg, R. J. (1997). Managerial intelligence: Why IQ isn't enough. *Journal of Management, 23,* 475–493. http://dx.doi.org/10.1016/S0149-2063(97)90038-6

Steward, J. (1972). *Theory of culture change: The methodology of multilinear evolution.* Urbana: University of Illinois Press.

Stewart, Q. T., & Dixon, J. C. (2010). Is it race, immigrant status, or both? An analysis of wage disparities among men in the United States. *International Migration Review, 44,* 173–201. http://dx.doi.org/10.1111/j.1747-7379.2009.00802.x

Stuetzer, M., Obschonka, M., & Schmitt-Rodermund, E. (2013). Balanced skills among nascent entrepreneurs. *Small Business Economics, 41,* 93–114. http://dx.doi.org/10.1007/s11187-012-9423-2

Surowiecki, J. (2010, October 11). Later. What does procrastination tell us about ourselves? *New Yorker,* 110–113. Retrieved from http://www.newyorker.com/magazine/2010/10/11/later

Taplin, S. H., Foster, M. K., & Shortell, S. M. (2013). Organizational leadership for building effective health care teams. *Annals of Family Medicine, 11,* 279–281. http://dx.doi.org/10.1370/afm.1506

Taylor, L. M. (1997). The relation between resilience, coaching, coping skills training, and perceived stress during a career-threatening milestone. *Dissertation Abstracts International, 58*(5), 2738.

Thompson, J. D. (1967). *Organizations in action.* New York, NY: McGraw-Hill.

Thornton, G. C., III, Hollenbeck, G. P., & Johnson, S. K. (2010). Selecting leaders: Executives and high potentials. In J. L. Farr & N. T. Tippins (Eds.), *Handbook of employee selection* (pp. 823–840). New York, NY: Routledge.

Thornton, G. C., III, Rupp, D. E., & Hoffman, B. J. (2015). *Assessment center perspectives for talent management strategies* (2nd ed.). New York, NY: Routledge.

Tosi, H. L., Misangyi, V. F., Fanelli, A., Waldman, D. A., & Yammarino, F. J. (2004). CEO charisma, compensation, and firm performance. *The Leadership Quarterly, 15,* 405–420. http://dx.doi.org/10.1016/j.leaqua.2004.02.010

Ucbasaran, D., Westhead, P., & Wright, M. (2011, April). Why serial entrepreneurs don't learn from failure. *Harvard Business Review, 89,* 26.

Uniform Guidelines on Employee Selection Procedures, 41 C.F.R. § 60.3. (1978). Retrieved from http://uniformguidelines.com/uniguideprint.html

United Nations High Commissioner for Refugees. (2015). *Syrian regional refugee response.* Retrieved from http://data.unhcr.org/syrianrefugees/country.php?id=224

U.S. Department of Labor. (2012). *The African-American labor force in the recovery.* Washington, DC: Author. Retrieved from http://www.dol.gov/_sec/media/reports/BlackLaborForce/BlackLaborForce.pdf

Van Iddekinge, C. H., Putka, D. J., & Campbell, J. P. (2011). Reconsidering vocational interests for personnel selection: The validity of an interest-based selection test in relation to job knowledge, job performance, and continuance intentions. *Journal of Applied Psychology, 96*, 13–33. http://dx.doi.org/10.1037/a0021193

Van Iddekinge, C. H., Raymark, P. H., & Roth, P. L. (2005). Assessing personality with a structured employment interview: Construct-related validity and susceptibility to response inflation. *Journal of Applied Psychology, 90*, 536–552. http://dx.doi.org/10.1037/0021-9010.90.3.536

Van Iddekinge, C. H., Roth, P. L., Raymark, P. H., & Odle-Dusseau, H. N. (2012). The criterion-related validity of integrity tests: An updated meta-analysis. *Journal of Applied Psychology, 97*, 499–530. http://dx.doi.org/10.1037/a0021196

Vukotich, G. (2014). Problems and pitfalls with 360° feedback. *Business Studies Journal, 6*, 103–120.

Wade, J. B., Porac, J. F., & Pollock, T. G. (1997). Worth, words, and the justification of executive pay [Special issue]. *Journal of Organizational Behavior, 18*(S1), 641–664. http://dx.doi.org/10.1002/(SICI)1099-1379(199711)18:1+<641::AID-JOB910>3.0.CO;2-M

Wai, J., Lubinski, D., & Benbow, C. P. (2009). Spatial ability for STEM domains: Aligning over 50 years of cumulative psychological knowledge. *Journal of Educational Psychology, 101*, 817–835. http://dx.doi.org/10.1037/a0016127

Wales, W. J., Patel, P. C., & Lumpkin, G. T. (2013). In pursuit of greatness: CEO narcissism, entrepreneurial orientation, and firm performance variance. *Journal of Management Studies, 50*, 1041–1069. http://dx.doi.org/10.1111/joms.12034

Walker, A. (2007). Group work in higher education: Are introverted students disadvantaged? *Psychology Learning & Teaching, 6*, 20–25. http://dx.doi.org/10.2304/plat.2007.6.1.20

Walsh, J. P. (2008). CEO compensation and the responsibilities of the business scholar to society. *The Academy of Management Perspectives, 22*, 26–33.

Watzlawick, P., Weakland, J., & Fisch, R. (1974). *Change: Principles of problem formation and problem resolution.* New York, NY: Norton.

Weick, K. E. (1979). *The social psychology of organizing* (2nd ed.). Reading, MA: Addison-Wesley.

White, J. K. (1979). The Scanlon Plan: Causes and correlates of success. *Academy of Management Journal, 22*, 292–312. http://dx.doi.org/10.2307/255591

White, R. P., & Shullman, S. L. (2012). Thirty years of global leadership training: A cross-cultural odyssey. *Consulting Psychology Journal: Practice and Research, 64*, 268–278. http://dx.doi.org/10.1037/a0031654

Winum, P. C., Nielsen, T. M., & Bradford, R. E. (2002). Assessing the impact of organizational consulting. In R. L. Lowman (Ed.), *Handbook of organizational consulting psychology: A comprehensive guide to theory, skills, and techniques* (pp. 645–667). San Francisco, CA: Jossey-Bass.

Woodman, R. W., Bingham, J. B., & Yuan, F. (2008). Assessing organization development and change interventions. In T. G. Cummings (Ed.), *Handbook of organization development* (pp. 187–216). Thousand Oaks, CA: Sage.

Wunder, R. S., Thomas, L. L., & Luo, Z. (2010). Administering assessments and decision-making. In J. L. Farr & N. T. Tippins (Eds.), *Handbook of employee selection* (pp. 377–398). New York, NY: Routledge.

Yang, Y., & Danes, S. M. (2015). Resiliency and resilience process of entrepreneurs in new venture creation. *Entrepreneurship Research Journal, 5,* 1–30. http://dx.doi.org/10.1515/erj-2013-0076

Zaleznik, A., & de Vries, M. K. (1976, Spring). What makes entrepreneurs entrepreneurial? *Business & Society Review,* 18–24.

Index

and communication patterns,
51–55
and definitions of group, 43–44
and developmental history of
groups, 46–51
interventions in, 57–59
organizational context for, 59–61
overview, 7–10, 43–61
Group leaders, 8. *See also* Leadership

Hackman, J. R., 96, 97
Hackman, Richard, 49, 57
Halfhill, T. R., 78
Harm, avoidance of (ethical issue),
112–114
"Hawthorne effect," 45
Hawthorne Electric Works, 45
Herndon, L., 103
Hiring, 26–27, 89–90
Hogan, J., 39, 89
Hogan, R., 39, 89
Homans, G., 43, 50
Hospitals, 76
Howard, A., 85
Howland, Alex, 56
Huff, J. W., 78
The Human Group (G. Homans), 44
*The Human Organization: Its
Management and Value*
(Rensis Likert), 65
Human resources professionals, 90

Immigrants, 103, 105
Incarceration, 103
Inceoglu, I., 108
Individual differences, 115
Individual-level consultation, 21–42
for assessment of psychopathology,
27–29
career assessment in, 21–26
career counseling, 37–41
case examples, 6–7

coaching, 29–37
for hiring and promotion
decisions, 26–27
onboarding, 41–42
overview, 4–7
retirement, 41–42
unemployment coaching, 41–42
Industrial–organizational (I-O)
psychology, 27, 29–31,
119, 138
Informed consent, 116–118
Institute for Social Research (ISR),
65, 73
Integrity, 86
Intelligence, 25, 85
International issues. *See* Multicultural
and international issues
Interventions
in group consulting work, 57–59
in organizational consulting,
75–79
Intervention Theory and Method
(C. Argyris), 59
Interviews, group assessment, 56
Introversion, 86
I-O psychology. *See* Industrial–
organizational psychology
ISR (Institute for Social Research),
65, 73

James, L. R., 88–89
Johnson, D. A., 58, 78

Kahn, R. L., 64
Kaiser, R. B., 39, 89
Katz, D., 64

Leadership, 81–99
abilities for, 84–85, 88
elements of, 82–83
and entrepreneurship, 93–95
in groups, 52–53, 95–97
management vs., 90–93

About the Author

Rodney L. Lowman, PhD, is currently a distinguished professor in the California School of Professional Psychology and is past provost/vice president of academic affairs and past acting president of Alliant International University.

Dr. Lowman has authored or edited nine books and monographs, published more than 130 scholarly and professional publications, and given hundreds of professional presentations all over the world. His previous works include *Internationalizing Multiculturalism: Expanding Professional Competencies in a Globalized World; Handbook of Organizational Consulting Psychology; The Ethical Practice of Psychology in Organizations* (2nd ed.); *The Clinical Practice of Career Assessment: Abilities, Interests, and Personality; Counseling and Psychotherapy of Work Dysfunctions;* and *Pre-Employment Screening: A Guide to Professional Practice.* Dr. Lowman has served as editor of *Consulting Psychology Journal: Practice and Research,* the flagship journal in the field of consulting psychology, currently is the series editor of the APA Fundamentals of Consulting Psychology book series, and was founding editor of *The Psychologist-Manager Journal.* He has also served on the editorial boards of other journals and has lectured widely both in the United States and abroad on professional ethics, consulting psychology, career assessment and counseling, and counseling and psychotherapy of work dysfunctions.

Dr. Lowman is a Fellow of the American Psychological Association (APA), Divisions 12 (Society of Clinical Psychology), 13 (Society of

Consulting Psychology), 14 (Society for Industrial and Organizational Psychology), 17 (Society of Counseling Psychology), and 52 (International Psychology), and he is a Diplomate of the American Board of Assessment Psychology. He also heads the Scientific Advisory Board of Leadership Worth Following, a Dallas-based consulting firm. Dr. Lowman is past president of the Society of Consulting Psychology and the Society for Psychologists in Management. He has served as Research Domain Leader and as elected APA Council representative for the Society of Consulting Psychology, and later as elected APA Council representative for the Society for Industrial and Organizational Psychology. He was the inaugural elected chair of the APA's Council Leadership Team and in this role served as a nonvoting participant on APA's Board.

Dr. Lowman has received many honors and recognitions for his professional work, including the Richard Kilburg Service Award from the Society of Psychologists in Management, the Service Award from the Society for Consulting Psychology, and the International–Multicultural Provost's Award from Alliant International University. He is a licensed psychologist in California and currently resides in San Diego with his spouse, clinical psychologist Dr. Linda Richardson. Their daughter is a writer and entrepreneur who lives in New York, where she is attending Cornell University's "Cornell Tech" MBA program.